The Culinary Dangers
of
Rural France...
and Other Stories

*The memoirs and musings of
a slightly deranged Englishman*

John Beadon

ISBN: 9798656344302

PublishNation
www.publishnation.co.uk

CONTENTS

PART TWO – AFRICAN ADVENTURES

Foreword

I have been lucky to lead an unusually full and adventuresome life.

I have probably spent a total of 10 months doing office work, over a working lifetime of over 50 years, and I will be eternally grateful that I have been able to steer clear of offices so much.

I spent years working in aquariums and dolphinariums. I caught fish to stock tanks, I dived in unexplored places for small fish and coral, I caught and trained fur-seals, sealions and dolphins. This work took me to wonderful places, such as the then-deserted beaches and reefs of Zululand in the 1970s, the cold waters of the Cape of Good Hope, the tropical paradise of Mozambique, and the wilds of the Red Sea off the coast of the Sinai Peninsula.

In the life that followed this, from the age of 30 onwards, I sailed. I ran sailing schools; I delivered yachts all over the Indian and Atlantic oceans; I ran a fast motorboat in the southern part of the Red Sea, living a life of excitement and danger for a year. I was contracted to sail some of the loveliest yachts imaginable, to destinations of incredible beauty. I grew with the yachting industry, and ran large superyachts for obscenely wealthy owners. I chartered for the rich, the famous, the infamous and, sometimes, the downright despicable.

During this fun-filled life, I fell in love frequently, sometimes sensibly, sometimes foolishly, but always exuberantly. I was married three times, and have managed to remain friends (or at least not enemies) with all three ladies. Very late in life, I have discovered the joy of sharing my time with a partner whom I adore, and who manages to always give me enough rope with which to choke (if not actually hang myself). She also seems to always understand why I sometimes need to spend time by myself, something that my psyche demands from time to time.

Later in life, I started writing purely for my own enjoyment, but now, at the age of 70, I would like to share these scribblings with anyone who enjoys laughter.

The short stories are divided into four sections: "Flavours of France", about my life here in Puget-Théniers; "African Adventures", which is chiefly about South Africa; "Bloody Boats" – self-explanatory! and "English Tales".

There is a certain amount of poetic licence in some of the stories, and some of them are drawn completely from my imagination, (thanks to many a sleepless night spent imaging 'what if...?'), but the vast majority are accounts of my own experiences and the experiences of others: happenings at sea; around South Africa; or in the village of Puget-Théniers in the Alpes-Maritimes region of France, where I purchased a run-down shepherd's cottage on an unkempt acre of land. This is now my home (and the source of a liberal supply of characters for my stories).

John Beadon
April 2020

Acknowledgements

I would like to thank all the characters, named and unnamed, who have appeared in these stories. They have stamped their idiosyncrasies indelibly on my mind.

Most thanks must go to Jackie Fothergill, whose patience and attention to detail in proofreading and editing my scribbles, has helped to make the stories readable.

PART ONE

FLAVOURS OF FRANCE

The Les Tréniers Spook

I live in a small stone house in the foothills of the Alpes-Maritimes region of France. The house is a converted 'bergerie' or shepherd's cottage, and it is very old, probably around 250 years. It had been extended from the original 'one up and one down' configuration, and boasted two bedrooms, a bathroom and a kitchen when I bought it. I have modernised it considerably, and added a second bathroom as well as patios, a new fireplace, a better kitchen and other necessities for a comfortable life.

I bought the place from a local hotelier who had only owned it for a year before having a heart attack. The driveway is 400 metres long, uphill all the way, and I bloody nearly had a heart attack myself when I first walked up.

The hotelier had bought the house from the Faccini family, who seemed to have owned most of the land in the area for generations. They decided to sell the house and twenty acres of land on the death of the old grandmother, who had lived there since her husband's demise. The Faccini clan all remember her with great affection, and frequently boast of her prowess as a great cook.

I live here on my own and, though I enjoy cooking for myself, I do so in a typically male way. I cook very simply, with as little effort as is required for the best result.

Imagine my confusion one night about six months after taking up residence, when I woke up in the early hours of the morning to the devastatingly delicious odour of 'Magret de Canard', or was it possibly 'Foie de Veau'? Anyway, it was enough to get me out of bed and padding around at three in the morning, trying to locate the source of this olfactory bonanza. I headed down the steep stairs, and the smell suddenly disappeared.

Now, I must explain that my nearest neighbour is about five hundred metres distant, and that it would be quite impossible for cooking smells to reach me from their house. Besides which, they are both so unbelievably skinny that I am certain they would never cook anything delicious. About two months later the same thing happened, and again the wonderful odours disappeared as soon as I started investigating.

Some time afterwards, I happened to be speaking to Bruno Faccini, the grandson of the old widow, and mentioned to him these strange occurrences. Bruno went a little pale, and told me that his grandmother had adored cooking, especially for her family on religious and other holidays, when all the sons and their families would gather at the bergerie for a family reunion.

Ok. So I had a ghost living with me in my house. At least it was not a malevolent spirit who caused chaos and terrified people and, very importantly, she always seemed to use her own ingredients for her mammoth cooking sessions. I decided that I was definitely blessed to have such a wonderfully domesticated spook.

Last week, on the 6th of January, I awoke at about two in the morning to the most unbelievably delicious smell. I lay in bed and salivated at the odour of what I thought to be a 'Daube de Sanglier', a wild boar stew made with Cèpes and other wild mushrooms. I happily turned over and went back to sleep, only to waken again at three, this time to the impression that I was in a bakery, so sharp were the wafts of rising, hot dough or possibly the crust of something delicious turning golden in an oven. As always, the smell disappeared after a little while, and again I went back to sleep.

The next day I was talking to one of my neighbours, Gilbert, and recounting to him the night's alarums. Gilbert turned very pale and surreptitiously crossed himself. I must admit that I took a couple of steps backwards—Gilbert crossing himself is likely to cause a lightning strike in his near vicinity, as he is a most unholy man.

Gilbert was of the opinion that the old lady had been cooking for the Feast of the Epiphany: 6th January is the day that French families get together and eat huge amounts of good traditional fare, at the end of which they eat the Galette des Rois, a sort of cake that is only baked at this time.

Me? I feel that my house has an extra little 'je ne sais quoi' that makes it even more special.

Go for it Granny Faccini!

January 2014

My Friend Gilbert

I have a neighbour called Gilbert Albano, who lives about three-quarters of a kilometre from me. He is a small gnome of a man, around sixty-two years old, as tough as old boot leather, who is convinced—despite his very bald head, his lack of height and his false teeth—that every female between the ages of twenty and sixty in the area is secretly dreaming of passionate affairs with him.

This is certainly just a harmless 'Walter Mitty' side of his character.

He is extremely careful with his money, but is generous with his time and knowledge. He grew up in Puget-Théniers, one of seven children, and left school at the age of eleven in order to start work and to help the family funds. The Albano clan are legion. There are so many Albanos around, that some of them don't even know some of the other Albanos.

About ten years ago Gilbert helped me to build a new bathroom, for which I paid him an agreed fee, and we talked a lot while mixing concrete, laying tiles and so forth. (I should really say that Gilbert talked, and I listened, as he seems to be able to talk non-stop for hours. I truly wonder when he draws breath.) He told me his entire life history, including the enormous number of local ladies whose favours he had turned down. He said that he was concerned that they were after his money, which is not so laughable, as he has built a very lovely house with his own hands, and it must be worth a packet. Gilbert lives alone, having divorced his wife some twenty years ago, but his son and daughter come and visit him each weekend. Both offspring are in their twenties, and I think that such filial constancy shows that Gilbert is a good man, who is truly respected and loved by his kids.

There is a stable in the corner of his property, housing an old mare called Bambi, a much younger gelding called Thunder, and a brain-dead donkey called Fennel. These three are boarded out to me for about six weeks each summer, so that they can crop the grass in my field. Behind the stables there is a coop containing about ten chickens, who lay the most enormous eggs. After much trial and error, Gilbert managed to find a mute rooster, who soundlessly struts his stuff. (I suspect that the preceding roosters were all turned into tasty stews and pies.)

There is a sign on Gilbert's fence that reads: 'ATTENTION CHIENS BIZARRES', and the sign is very truthful: there are two dogs, and they are both extremely bizarre. They are crossbreeds with a high percentage of Andalusian sheep dog in their veins. This means that they are huge beasts, with long shaggy coats, and they both slobber revoltingly.

A year or two ago, Gilbert found himself a very sophisticated lady-friend from Nice. Said lady was invited to come and spend the weekend with Gilbert during a long, hot summer. She duly arrived on the Friday afternoon in her Smart car, carrying a small Yorkshire terrier (complete with pink bow atop its head) under her arm. The lady put the Yorkie on the ground and the two behemoth dogs came up and sniffed at it. Gilbert remonstrated, saying that she should bring the little fellow around to the back of the house with her, but she poo-pooed the idea, saying that they were all dogs and would soon sort it out between them. The humans then left for the swimming pool, where the ever-ready Gilbert had a bottle of champagne waiting on ice, leaving a very worried little Yorkie straining his neck to look up at two beasts the size of small cars.

Gilbert told me later that he had heard a sound, emanating from the other side of the house, that did not bode well for his future relationship, so he left his lady-friend by the pool and scurried around to the front. He was greeted by the appalling sight of the little Yorkie in two pieces, as the two monsters had pulled it apart. Gilbert, thinking that the lady would probably be in extremis but might like to take the small cadaver for burial, put the two halves in a bag.

A transparent plastic bag.

Gilbert told me this story in wounded tones, saying that he couldn't understand why the lady seemed so bitter with him. I did try to point out that possibly a cardboard box, or some other container that didn't publicly advertise the savagery that had occurred, might have been more suitable.

Needless to say, the liaison came to a very abrupt end.

***

Gilbert has a distressing habit, which seems to be shared by most males living in this part of the French countryside. He makes 'saucisson' during the winter. This gastronomic perversion is made using wild boar meat, pork fat, garlic and certain herbs. The mixture is forced into a sausage skin, wrapped in hessian, and hung from the roof of a small and very smelly little shed. The long and odiferous bundles hang there for around six months, and eventually become fairly firm and dry.

I had gone to visit Gilbert to borrow a soldering-iron—he has every tool known to man in his cavernous garage—and he seemed very excited.

"La saucisse est prêt!" he shouted happily, "Il faut que tu la goûtes." I nervously followed him into the small shed, and he whipped out a knife from his back pocket. He sawed off a large disc of sausage, and handed it to me to peel and try. I am happy to eat just about anything, but Gilbert's handiwork is on the small list of no-no.

I pretended to take a bite, and hoped that in the limited light of the shed he would not notice. I was sure that I could get the loathsome morsel into my pocket somehow. I chewed energetically on nothing, while hiding the disgusting bit of offal in my hand, when I felt a large and wet nose investigating my hand. The older of the two dogs accepted the sausage with glee, while I carried on miming enjoyment and made appreciative noises.

Gilbert was delighted, and immediately cut me another, even thicker slab. I motioned to some boxes at the back of the shed, and asked what he kept in them. As soon as he turned his head, I whipped my hand behind me again, while chewing ecstatically on nothing but saliva. Again, the huge and hairy brute took the piece of sausage and swallowed it whole. I thanked Gilbert profusely, and took my leave. On arriving home, I washed my hands and decided that I had had a very lucky escape.

To this day, whenever I visit Gilbert, the great lumbering beast of a dog greets me with incredible fervour, and with a certain look in his eye that says, 'where is the sausage?'

August 2018

Lunch in June

I am home. After four months of dealing with irritable owners, avaricious suppliers, frankly abusive yacht managers, and whingeing crew, I am back in my decidedly monastic home, and as happy as a pig in pig manure.

It is Saturday today, and a good day to visit the village, where I purchased a beautiful rotisserie chicken, a ripe mango, and a couple of avocados. I also picked up a bottle of fine Provence rosé and a bottle of red (for later).

The sun was shining, the gentle breeze was making the heavy branches of the plum tree sway, reminding me that I must pick plums this afternoon and make some jam—waste not, want not.

I settled down in the kitchen and decided how I would prepare my lunch. First, I denuded the chicken, ripping every piece of flesh off the carcass (which would be fed to the foxes later that night). I selected the meat from the legs and wings for my lunch, wrapping up the rest for future use. I cut and buttered some baguette de campagne, which was warm and very fresh. Now, for the 'healthy' side of the meal: I cut up one of the avocados, which was perfect, chopped some small fresh plum tomatoes and added them to the avo. Olive oil, soy sauce, pepper and salt finished the salad.

Or did it?

No. There was something missing. I ventured out to the herb garden and picked a couple of sprigs of fresh basil, took them into the kitchen, chopped them finely, and added them to the salad.

With the bottle of rosé opened and tasted—magnificent!—the feast was ready.

I settled down at the table outside my kitchen door, sat back and knew that I was master of all that I surveyed – it really makes one feel good!

I diligently ate my way through the whole meal, chicken, bread and salad, washed it all down with the crisp rosé, and then smiled at life, replete and happy.

Something in the back of my head was telling me that there had been a slightly different and intriguing taste to the salad. I thought for a while, but there was nothing new that I had spontaneously added. I picked up the salad bowl, and searched through the dregs.

VOILA!!

I (inadvertently, I assure the reader), when plucking the heads of basil, had somehow taken into the kitchen a green grasshopper, who, bless his long, spiky legs, had been chopped finely with the basil.

There was a single spiky leg left in the salad bowl as evidence.

The insouciant flavour that this addition imbued to the salad has necessitated a name being given to it.

From now on it shall be known as Salade a la Cigale.

Bon Appetit!!

June 2015

The Bar in Puget

Today is Friday, the day that I normally visit Madame Nadine who runs the small grocery shop, and then go next door to her Spanish husband the butcher, where I buy sheep's cheese and chicken. It is also a good day to drop in to the local bar and catch up on the village news.

Today was again a bright day, frost glistening under the sun, and I watched the local gendarmes, all dressed in their best uniforms, coming from the church – it transpired that today was the day of St. Lucien, the patron saint of cops. There was some low murmuring suggesting that it was an ideal day to stage a robbery somewhere, as all the gendarmes were out, looking good and drinking copious amounts of wine. I wandered into the bar and sat down next to Jean-Claude, an ex-legionnaire who supports the bar almost single-handedly. Behind the bar today was Coline: I must tell you about Coline.

Coline is all of about eighteen years old and absolutely delightful. She has long tawny hair that is always in slight disarray – to an ageing lecher she appears to have just been hauled out of bed. She has a dramatically pretty face, with a peppering of freckles across a nose that wrinkles slightly when she laughs – which she does a lot. Her taut and undeniably lush young body is usually clad in tight jeans and clinging sweaters. There is always a hush as she reaches for a bottle of pastis from above the bar, and a collective sigh as the twin masterpieces of her unrestrained breasts settle back in place. She seems to be totally unaware of this constant leering and panting from the assembled male population of the village, but I suspect that as she is (1) female, and (2) pretty, she knows exactly what she is doing to the collective blood pressure of the crowd – all girls do.

I was just finishing my 'petit rouge', and wondering how to get Jean-Claude to buy his round for a change, when in walked Christophe Segura, the local plumber. Christophe is a likeable character, about 35 years old, married with three children, but with a bold and roving eye. He is dark haired and bearded, thanks to his Spanish parentage, and plays an important part in the social life of the village. Besides helping out with setting up stalls for the Christmas and Easter fairs, he always takes the part of Père Noël (Father Christmas) for the children's party at the Salle des Fêtes.

When he walked in it was obvious that he had just come from another location where drink was served, and it turned out to be the gendarmes' mess, where he had imbibed a lot of wine. I offered him a drink and he loudly thanked me, before turning to the rest of the assembled men and insisting that they all buy him drinks as recompense for his heroism.

When asked what heroic deeds he had performed, he explained that it was his upcoming stint as Père Noël that was heroic: apparently some of the children were really revolting, and some of the parents downright threatening. Someone made the observation that he had been seen in previous years trying to coax some of the younger mothers onto his knee, no doubt merely to ask what they would like from Père Noël, n'est ce pas?

There was a lot more banter, and the atmosphere in the bar grew ever louder and jollier. It happened that the open bottle of wine was finished, and Coline turned her back on the patrons, bending down from the waist to get a new bottle from the lower cupboard. This is where the trouble started.

Christophe was heard to enunciate quite clearly, "Sacré Dieu, sa derrière est absolument parfait!"

Now, just telling the assembly that Coline's bottom was absolutely perfect was not too terrible, but he then carried on in a hushed tone, voicing his incredible desire to have Coline perch her flawless backside upon his knee, and that he would give her every toy in his sack, with gusto, if she would.

I have used great restraint in my translation of what Christophe actually said, but it was enough to leave the entire bar in a stunned silence.

Coline reacted surprisingly for such a happy girl: she whipped round and launched herself over the bar, boxing Christophe's ears with both hands. At the same time she threatened, at the top of her voice, to go to his house and repeat to Madame Segura every disgraceful word that he had uttered.

Christophe wilted. He stood there abjectly, wringing his hands and begging the enraged girl not to do so, but to accept his grovelling apology.

Coline dried a glass while considering his sorrowful figure, eventually giving him a blinding smile and suggesting that perhaps he should buy a round and then leave a decent tip. There was a roar of approval from the crowd, and the subject was forgotten.

Never a dull moment …

November 2011

Rendezvous des Voisins

Puget-Théniers is a small town in the Alpes-Maritimes district of France, and Nice is the biggest nearby city, only fifty kilometres to the south. The town boasts a population of around 1800, most of whom are vociferously right-wing French, with very little time for 'big city' clothes, habits or ideas.

I live on a road outside the town called Les Trenières, which is a small, winding tarred track leading to the water tower above the town. There are only fourteen houses on the whole four-kilometre length of the road, so it will not surprise the reader that I was astounded when my house was awarded street number 817. I asked one of the dragons who run the local post office how this could possibly be correct. She scratched her moustachioed upper lip, and rather ashamedly explained that the house numbers were actually the crow-flying distance of each house from the post office.

Unreal.

Les Trenières seems to have attracted some pretty bizarre and exotic characters as residents. There is the seldom-seen and very secretive retired Russian general, name unknown. The artist, Conil, who has not touched a brush in twelve years as a protest against a Paris gallery which accused him of plagiarism. Gilbert, the local clinic handyman, who once cut off half his foot with a chainsaw. I feel very at home here, and I have actively helped along any rumours that hint at my own eccentricity.

Every year we have a 'Rendezvous des Voisins', an evening when the neighbours get together, sometimes seeing each other for the first time in twelve months. I have never seen all the denizens of the street make the evening, but there is usually a turnout of around twenty people, including children and visiting relations.

This year was a classic. We met down at the T-junction and, in the road, set up two long tables which were soon groaning under plates of food and bottles of wine. I brought some pâté, a baguette and a box of local rosé wine, but many of the local matrons had excelled themselves. There were trays of 'socca' (a local pizza base) covered in deep-fried onions, strange flat omelettes filled with local dried 'mystery' meat, (which I have long suspected to be donkey), and too many other delicacies to mention. There were also 'gateaux'- enough sugar to make a diabetic walk away immediately.

The local wives seemed to treat this as a sort of competition – 'see how well I look after MY man!', and they dressed the part too, with all sorts of jaw-dropping ensembles being shown off, often not to great advantage.

I had decided to walk the kilometre from my house, as the evening was balmy and the sky clear and, having left too early to avoid being late, I was the first to arrive. I sat down in the grass on the verge and opened my rosé. Next to arrive was François with his wife and two veg. His wife is called Adélie, and I am sure that in her teens she must have looked sweet and 'gamine', but unfortunately in her early forties she had become thin-lipped and shrewish. The two children were normal French kids, a pretty pre-teen girl and a spotty teen boy, incredibly badly behaved, loud, and inclined to show no respect whatsoever to senior citizens. Adélie had brought a load of food, upon which the children descended like a couple of vultures shrieking at each other, while their mother tried to beat them off.

In dribs and drabs the rest of the company arrived. Conil lumbered in carrying a cool-box filled with his home-made and definitely illegal liqueurs, Serge arrived with his young twin boys, who I am certain are going to end up in a prison for young offenders, probably before their eleventh birthday. He was accompanied also by his wife, the incomparable Angélique.

Now Angélique was certainly a beauty of the village a decade or so ago, and she still turns heads very easily. Serge is easy-going and relaxed about it, but his wife, with her strawberry blond mane and big green eyes seems to ignite a rather base and savage sort of lust in all the other men around.

On this particular evening she had spared nothing when dressing for the event. She was a tall woman, with extremely generous curves, and these curves had been pushed, pummelled and forced into clothing that was possibly a trifle small. Her child-bearing hips and her opulent buttocks had been poured into a pair of black Spandex stretch pants, while her spectacular and huge breasts had been uplifted and sculpted by a brassiere of truly heroic design. She had then chosen an off-the-shoulder white jersey-fabric top, which allowed the awe-struck neighbours uninterrupted views of a cleavage that would have had a corpse licking its lips. The ensemble was completed by a pair of gold sandals with high heels, on which Angélique tottered and giggled, while leaning on the arm of the nearest male.

I thought Conil, at age eighty-plus, was going into cardiac arrest. He stared at Angélique while gripping the edge of the table, muttering something incomprehensible, which was surely either a prayer or an obscenity.

Cedric and his wife Cécile, who normally showed no emotion, were both mesmerized at the sight of Angélique. This surprised me, as the only other time that I had seen Cedric so enthralled was when I found him watching a flock of young sheep with what can only be described as a rather unhealthy interest.

David and Nathalie arrived late with their brood of disgusting offspring, both of whom were riding their scooters at breakneck speed down the sloping road. Nathalie, ever the concerned parent, immediately gave the children as much to eat as it was possible to put on a plate.

The conversation eddied around the tables, more wine was opened, food was eaten and praised, and the whole time the male eyes covetously glanced to where Angélique was. She could not stay seated, and kept getting up to talk to someone, or to get a particular delicacy for herself or her husband, and each time she turned and presented her roiling derrière to the assembled company there was a low rumbling of appreciation.

The standard of decorum slowly degenerated; Conil produced his 'Génépi', a vicious liqueur made from eau-de-vie and the petals of a small flower found in the Alps. I suspect that the drink is around 70-proof and designed specifically to make one blind. One of Nathalie's boys ate too much chocolate cake, rode his scooter furiously, and then vomited copiously into his mother's lap. He was swatted off and told to go and wash his face, but Nathalie stayed, and the gentle odour of child-sick pervaded the area.

I noticed François in deep conversation with Angélique, and automatically looked for Adélie, to see what her reaction was. Now compared to Angélique, poor Adélie was a very poor piece of womanhood, I have seen better 'tits 'n ass' on one of the local snakes. Adélie was watching her husband through slitted eyes, grinding her teeth and ripping her paper napkin to shreds with the hands of a madwoman.

In a moment of near-silence, Adélie's voice came out in a sibilant hiss, "Sale pute!" she told Angélique.

Well, even in the closest of communities, calling your neighbour a dirty whore is a no-no. Angélique stood up straight, and told her husband to take her home immediately. Poor Serge slugged back the last of his wine, shrugged his shoulders, called "Bonne nuit!" to all, and took his wife by the elbow. There was a collective sigh, and Conil looked close to tears. The rest of the wives gathered around Adélie and told her how right she had been to say something.

I decided that it was time for me to leave, before anything else happened. I bade everyone goodnight and set off up the hill with my pâté still intact – no one had been interested in it.

I heard nothing of the wildlife around me in the dark, and I suspect that one whiff of the wine, Génépi, socca and all the other things that I had eaten, would be enough to terrify the meanest wild boar.

The joys of eccentric rural France!

July 2012

The Continuing Tale of Angélique

It has taken many days for the gentle inhabitants of Les Trenières to get over the disastrous end to the recent 'Rendezvous': Angélique has been ignored by the majority of the womenfolk, and their husbands are definitely too scared to be seen talking to her—just imagine what Adélie would do to François if she discovered that he had conversed again with this scarlet woman!

Serge, Angélique's husband, seems to be completely unaware of the seething cauldron of jealousy and contempt that his wife has managed to provide for the village. And Angélique? She also seems to be totally unaffected by the looks, asides and whispers to which the local matrons resort as soon as she appears.

Conil, Gilbert and I, however, can do and say as we please, as we are not encumbered with female companionship and therefore don't run the risk of having our eyes scratched out for talking to the poor woman.

A few days ago, I was in the local Carrefour supermarket buying groceries and wine, when I was confronted by Angélique and her shopping trolley. She gave me a delighted smile and, as is the French custom, planted 'les bises' (kisses) on my cheeks. We spoke briefly, and then continued down our separate aisles to gather our merchandise. There were a couple of young 'pompiers' (firemen), who were entranced with their first view of Angélique, and started to follow her around the shop, feasting their eyes on her generous curves.

This particular day Angélique was wearing a pink vest, which did virtually nothing to cover her stupendous breasts, a pair of calf-length denims that had to have been painted on, and bright red platform sandals that matched her lipstick. Her red-gold hair was tied back in a cheeky ponytail and her finger and toenails were painted a soft coral colour.

All in all, intimidatingly magnificent.

I noticed that even the cashiers, normally a cheerful and friendly bunch of women, all stared at her with expressions that told of their disquiet that this woman shared the same village as their husbands.

Angélique was certainly all woman, and a lot of woman at that.

I had finally chosen the wines that I wanted, and realised that I had forgotten to buy cheese, so I carried my basket back towards the open-fronted cooler where the cheeses were displayed. I saw the two firemen still walking around with the same amount of produce in their basket, and deduced that they were no longer shopping, but were still following Angélique. I turned the corner past the bread section and stopped, aghast and appalled.

Angélique was bending over the lower of the cheese shelves, and I realised what she was actually wearing.

I think that past the age of about eighteen, girls should not try to wear 'hipster' jeans, and ladies of the opulent proportions that Angélique possessed should be prevented from wearing them by law.

I was confronted by the straining seams of the hipster jeans barely containing Angélique's prodigious buttocks, and, horror of horrors, said jeans had slid down to reveal the wisp of fabric that made up the sky-blue thong that disappeared between the creamy white orbs of shimmering flesh.

The firemen had suddenly remembered that they had items to buy, and had disappeared, while I was rooted to the ground with horror, and any latent sexual dreams that I may have had vanished in a trice.

An elderly man walked by, stared at this vaguely pornographic picture, had a quick check around to make sure that his wife was not watching and, gesturing repeatedly with his hands (in a very French manner), mouthed the words, "Ooh la la!"

I managed to turn around a moment before Angélique stood up, and made my way sadly to the check-out. I would never again be able to behold Angélique in quite the same way as I had before—I had seen too much!

August 2012

Club 202

On the Route Nationale 202, which is the road leading from Nice to Digne, Grenoble, Gap and the Swiss border, there stands a very pretty old house on the left side of the road.

It is an imposing place overlooking the river Var, and was once part of the estate of a nearby château. It is an isolated building, very much on its own, with no neighbours for at least two kilometres in either direction. The house is typically Provençal in design, with two floors, all the windows covered with green painted wooden shutters, and a symmetrical and pleasing tiled roof.

It is situated between the villages of Villars-sur-Var to the south and Touët-sur-Var to the north; both are small places with tight populations and self-reliant inhabitants. In the late '90s the house had been leased to an Italian writer who was something of a recluse, and who was seldom seen in the villages. He was rumoured to do all his shopping down in Nice once a month, and to have a variety of different female guests staying with him from time to time. The only local to have seen the inside of the house in recent times was the local electrician, Christophe Bellat, who had done some repair work previously.

Jean-Michel Frambois was the plumber in the area, and he lived in Villars with his wife Claudine, a large, verbose and bossy woman and their three children. Jean-Michel drove the road between Villars and Touët at least four times per week in the course of his work, and always took note of the house on the corner.

One day when passing the house, he saw a sign that read 'A LOUE' – 'For Rent'. That evening he stopped into the bar in Touët for a beer on the way home and ran into Christophe, the electrician. They sat outside in the warm evening, sipping their beers and musing on the local happenings of the last week or so.

Jean-Michel mentioned to Christophe that the house on the bend was up for rent again, and they wondered what had happened to the Italian writer, had he run out of money? Had he run away with one of his numerous paramours? They finished their drinks and went their separate ways.

***

The next morning, a Saturday, Christophe was at the local supermarket, the Shoppe in Puget-Théniers, when he met Gilbert, the baker from Touët. Gilbert was bemoaning the fact that the local 'boules' club had lost its clubhouse, and that there was nowhere for the fellows to sit and have a drink away from the prying eyes of their wives.

Christophe was pensive over the family lunch, and was more than once spoken to sharply by his wife Sandrine, a faded beauty who never tired of telling Christophe that she had married beneath her station. In the afternoon Christophe used his mobile to call Jean-Michel and they agreed to meet in Puget-Théniers at three o'clock. They visited the estate agent whose name was on the 'To Rent' board at the house, and made some vague enquiries as to the price of the monthly rental and the length of the lease.

The young estate agent drove behind them down the 202 to the house, and unlocked the door. The interior was a trifle stuffy and musty, but it was clean and dry, the tiled hallway was magnificent, with a wide stairway leading to the upper floor.

Jean-Michel and Christophe bade farewell to the estate agent, promising to contact him on the Monday morning.

They immediately called Gilbert Valmy the baker, and Patrick Paysan the local 'notaire'. The four men met at the bar in Touët, and discussed the possibility of turning the house on the bend into a local 'Working Men's Club'. The rent was not excessive, and split between the four of them it was easily affordable. The estate agent had

21

remarked that the owner, a retired Paris businessman, seemed keen on the idea of letting the house to local tradesmen who might be interested in doing some work on the place in return for a reduced rental.

Using a paper napkin, they quickly listed what they would need to make the place truly habitable for their needs: fridges, chairs and tables, a television set, some garden furniture and a couple of beds for visiting friends. They all grinned at each other in a conspiratorial fashion, then lifted their glasses and in unison toasted, 'Le Club Deux Cent Deux'!

Thus began the scandal that reverberated around the area for years to come.

***

The four friends met with the estate agent on the Monday morning, signed a lease for a year, and gave the estate agent four 'prélèvament automatique' forms, allowing the bank to pay the rent on the 26th of each month. They also put out the word that they were looking for second-hand furnishings in good condition, and soon had replies from people in Annot, Entrevaux and even from Nice. All four had decided against telling their spouses about the enterprise, deciding that there would be less resistance if they waited until it was a 'fait accompli'.

Over the course of the next month, the house rapidly took shape as the 'Club 202'. One of the main advantages of the place was that the parking area was between the house and the river, and was therefore invisible from the road. This meant that the four founder members could come and unload bits and pieces completely unobserved by passers-by.

Patrick, the eldest of the four at fifty-eight years of age, met a large number of people through his work, and was a raconteur of some note. He sounded out a couple of other likely gentlemen, and then presented them to Jean-Michel, Christophe and Gilbert for their approval. Within three months the club had a membership of fourteen, made up of local tradesmen, retired gentlemen and professionals living in the area. The members, comprising the ten who were not founders of the club, paid a monthly subscription into a bank account opened by Patrick, and this was used to cover all ongoing costs. The 'honour' bar was stocked at a discount house in Nice once a month, and the mark-up on bar sales was kept to 10%: the small profit was also paid into the bank account.

***

During the warm summer months, a regular occurrence was the Saturday barbecue, which was usually attended by all the members. Meat was supplied by Florent, the local butcher, and the timing of the cooking depended on what match—soccer or rugby—was being played that afternoon. In the end, there was a unanimous vote to buy a second television so that both sports could be watched simultaneously.

The membership continued to grow, and there were the occasional disputes as to whose turn it was to do the cleaning and laundry, as this was done on three days a week by a rotating list of the members. There was enough cash in the bank account to get professional cleaning staff in, but the question was, from where? Although by now most members had divulged to their respective spouses or partners the existence of the club, the rule of no female visitors applied, and the members were loath to allow local women into the club, as it might be the 'thin end of the wedge'. In the end Patrick contacted a cleaning firm in Nice, which took on the contract, and delivered two ladies to the club on Mondays, Wednesdays and Fridays.

The wives of the members were quite content for the most part. Their menfolk were not hanging around the house, they were not staying away overnight, there were no women allowed into the club, so what was there to complain about?

***

One of the newest members was the local commandant of gendarmes, who had been invited to join in order to short-circuit any officious nonsense about liquor licensing or other imbecilic legalities.

Commandant Lebel was a striking and vigorous figure, an ex-soldier who had joined the police and risen very quickly to his present rank. He had been posted to the area only the previous year, and was blissfully happy there. His young wife, Estelle, was not. She would have preferred to have been living in Nice, Antibes or Cannes, close to her friends, close to the sea and the 'beautiful people' that inhabited the coast. Estelle was only thirty-one, and often felt that she had made a mistake marrying the Commandant, who was fifty-five. She was a curvaceous and flirtatious girl who turned heads easily, and enjoyed making Jacques Lebel show flashes of jealousy.

At the end of the summer, the club members organised a fishing competition in the Var at the bottom of the sloping grounds of the house. Any type of bait, lure or fly was allowed, but the fish had to be caught between the hours of nine o'clock in the morning and midday, on the last Saturday in August. All the fish caught would then be cooked on the barbecues for lunch along with the lamb chops supplied by Florent.

The weather on the selected day was magnificent, and altogether nine fish were caught in the allotted time. The members were lounging around on the patio, sipping pastis or beer, discussing the fishing and the afternoon's television sport, when there was a strident ringing of the bell at the front door.

It was Patrick Paysan who opened the door and was confronted by Estelle, the commandant's wife. She was dressed to kill in a skirt so short that it was hardly decent, a sleeveless shirt tied across her flat and bronzed midriff, her feet in cork-heeled thongs and her long strawberry blond hair tied back in a ponytail. She brushed past old Patrick and strode across the hallway towards the open French windows, swinging her hips and clacking her heels.

There was silence as she took stock of the many eyes that were watching her, and then made her way towards her husband, who was looking and feeling extremely uncomfortable.

"Eh bien mon cher!" she said, "So this is where all you old guys hang out."

Jacques quickly took her by the arm, "Please chérie, you are not allowed to be here, let me take you back to your car and I will follow you home." He tried to lead her to the door, but she shook his hand off.

"You stupid old goat, I only stopped to tell you that I am going to Cannes to meet my sister, and that I will not be back until Monday, so stay and play games with your little friends here!"

She looked at the horrified assembled members and licked her lips to make the lipstick shine, then continued, "I bet that in Cannes I will find a young man who prefers to spend time with me than with a bunch of boring old farts!"

With that she strode out of the front door and slammed it behind her. There was a very uncomfortable silence, and Jacques Lebel eventually broke it by laughing and saying to his friends, "Well, boring old farts, let me buy you each a drink?"

There was a hubbub of nervous laughter, and a couple of fellows came up and patted Jacques on the shoulder, while everyone else helped themselves to a drink from the bar. The rest of the afternoon passed with a slight cloud over it, but the sport on the television was good and the members all enjoyed themselves.

***

Commandant Lebel spent most of Sunday at the club, while as usual most of the other members dropped in for a drink after church and before lunch. On Monday there was still no sign of Estelle Lebel, and the junior gendarmes at the station remarked that the 'old man' was in a foul mood. Patrick phoned the commandant on Tuesday, and enquired whether Estelle had returned home, and if not, would Jacques like to have dinner with him, as his wife was visiting relations in Bourgogne. Jacques Lebel seemed much cheered by this interest in his wellbeing, and the two gentlemen enjoyed a good dinner at 'Chez Paul' in Touët.

After the meal, while enjoying a Calvados with their coffee, Jacques admitted that he had heard from Estelle, and that she had decided to stay with her sister on the coast for a while, to 'clear her mind'.

"So, mon vieux, it seems I will be a widower for my birthday in October, when I should be enjoying the love of a full-bodied woman," said Jacques with a sigh.

Patrick Paysan was a sympathetic man, and thought long into the night about his friend's distress. The next morning, he called the lady that ran the cleaning service in Nice, and had a long and intimate conversation with her.

On the next weekend, Patrick spoke to the other three founders of the club, trying to gauge their position when it came to doing something for the commandant. Gilbert was immediately in full support of his ideas, while Christophe and Jean-Michel took a little winning over. It helped that Christophe received a phone call from his wife, giving him hell for not finishing some chore around the house before leaving.

***

The club was by now extremely comfortable. Curtains had been hung wherever they were needed, the bar had a dartboard and a pool table, there was a 'smoking room', as, with winter approaching, it would soon be too cold to smoke outside. The four chimneys had been swept; Serge, one of the members, had brought in eight 'stairs' of firewood and stacked it in the woodshed. The five bedrooms were now fitted out for use by members or their guests. All were huge rooms, which now boasted queen-sized beds with brass bedsteads. They could be used if a member had imbibed too much and could not drive, or if there was friction at home which made life uncomfortable.

Jean-Michel had used some of his time and that of his apprentice, and the two upstairs bathrooms were now splendid. They had showers and baths, had been re-tiled where necessary, and heaters had been installed for the winter. The downstairs bathroom had been altered, and now boasted a 'pissoir' as well as the toilet.

The membership had been capped at twenty-five, but there were many locals who had put their names on the 'waiting list', and waited out each month with impatience, hoping for a summons to be examined by the committee for membership. Each member paid €500 to join the club, and then €50 per month as a membership fee. The bank account swelled slowly, but the money was always used with the agreement of the four founder members.

**

Patrick called a meeting of the founder members mid-week at the club, and they all arrived within minutes of each other. They poured drinks and sat down while Patrick started to outline what he had in mind for Jacques's birthday celebration.

"Mes braves," he began, "poor Jacques has been cuckolded by that young hussy of a wife. Estelle has taken up with a foreigner who sells yachts in Monaco, and she seems to have no intention of returning to Puget-Théniers. I would like to suggest that we make his birthday next month as memorable as possible in every way."

There was the sound of a car drawing up at the door, and Patrick motioned to the other three to stay seated as he went to greet the arrival. He returned a minute later with a glamorous and statuesque lady of around fifty years old.

"Messieurs, may I present Madame du Plessis." He smiled at their confusion as he introduced each of them. Madame du Plessis was the

27

lady who ran the cleaning company contracted to the club, and although they knew her name, they had never seen her before.

"Mes amis," continued Patrick, "Catherine du Plessis has been my very special friend for the last twenty years," he smiled and took her hand as he said this, so that there could be no doubt as to what he meant. "Catherine is going to help us to plan an evening of delights for the poor commandant, and she will be our contact in this endeavour."

Catherine had a wonderfully husky voice, and she started to lay out a few suggestions for the approval of the friends. The three local tradesmen were astounded. Firstly, their friend Patrick turned out to have a 'very special friend', and a stunning one at that, and then the stunning friend started blowing their little minds with ideas of great delight to entertain Jacques Lebel on his birthday.

All three had lived pretty parochial lives, had married young, and had led lives of honest toil and care for their families. Here was a temptress telling them that there were available things of such beguiling sin and fun that their heads spun.

The discussion went on for about an hour, at the end of which the electrician, plumber and baker all took their leave with stuttering goodbyes to Catherine, and promises to Patrick to divulge nothing to their wives when they arrived home. Patrick and Catherine then opened a bottle of champagne from the bar, and retired to the largest guestroom for the night.

The preparations moved along quickly, with Catherine showing up at the club frequently. Sometimes there was a menu to peruse, sometimes photographs of beautiful girls wearing dancing costumes. Patrick was able to spend more time on the project than the other three, as he had a full office to carry on his work for him when he was otherwise occupied. His wife was not due back for another month, and this made it even easier for him.

The members were all apprised of what was happening, and told that they were all welcome to join in the celebrations that evening, that there would be a €100 entrance fee to be paid, and that secrecy was vital. All except two of the members bought into the evening: the two were devastated that they would be away on business that weekend. Commandant Jacques Lebel was told that his friends wished to give him a small birthday party at the club, and that he should be there at seven o'clock in the evening.

***

The Saturday earmarked for the birthday party finally arrived, and the afternoon was filled with comings and goings, vans and cars drew up to the house, were unloaded and then drove off. Inside, the fires had been lit to prepare to ward off the chill of the evening, and from the road one could hear music playing softly in the distance. Patrick was everywhere, as was Catherine, the two of them were busy laying the long table in the front room, checking on the catering company that had brought the food from Nice, and making sure that the entertainment was properly prepared. From the upstairs bedrooms came peals of girlish laughter, and every now and then Catherine would dart up to quieten things down.

The evening drew in, and it was deep dusk by the time the members started to arrive. Jean-Michel, Gilbert and Christophe arrived first, and were immediately put in charge of seating, music and the bar. The other members arrived in groups, and were quickly seated at the long table, until at last it was only the guest of honour that was missing. Christophe whistled to Jean-Michel as he saw the commandant's car pull up, and Jean-Michel prepared the correct track on the CD player. As Jacques Lebel opened the door, Edith Piaf's strong voice belted out the beginning of 'Milord', Jacques' favourite song. The surprise was complete, and the members all applauded as Jacques was led to his seat at the head of the table and handed a large pastis.

Jacques was still trying to get over his surprise when there was a shout from the men sitting along each side of the table, Jacques half turned in his seat, and saw what had excited everyone's attention.

A column of six girls, all dressed as Moulin Rouge dancers were advancing on the table, moving in time to the strains of Edith Piaf. They were scantily dressed and carried ostrich feather fans. The leader came towards Jacques. Her lovely face was smiling at him, and one eyelid dropped in an overt wink. The other girls separated down each side of the table, sometimes stroking their fans across the necks of the men who sat in awed excitement.

Jacques could not believe it when the leading dancer, who was endowed with a body to make a bishop rescind his vows, gently turned him in his chair, making room for her to perch on his lap. She had short, curly blond hair, huge blue eyes, and her bare shoulders were lightly bronzed by the sun. She was truly beautiful.

Jacques sat like a statue, never taking his eyes off this apparition who, putting a hand behind his neck, gently kissed the corner of his mouth, then breathed "Bon Anniversaire Monsieur le Commandant," into his ear.

The song came to an end, and there was a sudden silence, broken by a chuckle from a couple of the girls. The lead dancer slowly slipped from Jacques's lap, and he felt a genuine loss as she sashayed to the other end of the table, put her hands on her hips, and surveyed the stares of the men sitting at the table.

"Bon soir Messieurs!" She grinned at them, revelling in their popped eyes and open mouths. "Tonight we are going to party and make sure that the Commandant has the best birthday ever! D'accord?"

There was a buzz of sound from the assembled men, and then the music started playing again – this time it was Chris de Burgh singing "...Patricia the Stripper, she calls herself Delicia...", and one of the other girls jumped onto the table, swinging her hips and moving her shoulders to the music, while she slowly took off the top of her costume. She revealed the most perfect coral tipped breasts, stroked them with her hands and licked her lips while she gyrated on the table.

The members of Club 202 sat there in heaven. None of them had ever seen such perfect examples of womanhood, and all of them followed each movement of the dancer without blinking – just in case they missed something.

When that song finished, another girl climbed onto the table and danced to a different tune, climbing down when the song finished. None of them took the trouble to replace their missing brassieres, and eventually all six girls were proudly displaying their magnificent breasts.

The lead dancer, who had by now introduced herself as Gaëlle, was taking special care of Jacques, from time to time sitting on his lap again and feeding him delicate little morsels of food from the plates that now covered the table. The other girls circulated amongst the members, laughing and joking with them. Sometimes a man would be led out to dance with one of the girls, and his friends would all clap and cheer his expertise.

Many of the members had come to Jacques, shaken his hand and sorrowfully made their excuses before leaving for their family homes. The core party left numbered some eight men, including all four of the founder members. Catherine had appeared a little earlier, and was sitting with Patrick, sharing a bottle of champagne with him while they watched the party and smiled.

Jacques Lebel was sitting on his chair, Gaëlle was once again on his lap, and the other girls were all dancing together while the rest of the members clapped and cheered. Jacques stroked Gaëlle's cheek in wonder, and he murmured to her, "This is the most unbelievable birthday of my life, and I have had to wait until this age to experience it." Gaëlle smiled and lightly kissed him on the mouth, "Your birthday is not finished yet, mon brave, you still have your presents to open," she said.

The Commandant looked around in confusion, "Presents? I have presents as well? Where?" He asked the assembly. Gaëlle giggled and hugged his head to her naked bosom, "And what am I if not a present?" she asked wickedly. Jacques nearly passed out with a mixture of delight, embarrassment and surprise. "You are a present?" he stammered, and the beautiful girl took his head between her hands, stared into his eyes and whispered, "All six of us are your presents."

***

In Puget-Théniers there was an impromptu meeting taking place at the café. Present were seven women, all married to members of Club 202. They had met mostly by accident, and had started talking about the value of the club. They all agreed that it was wonderful that their husbands were not always hanging around the house, and that their home televisions were not always used for the boring sports programmes on Saturday afternoons. Some of them, however, were becoming fascinated by the chauvinistic rules of the club; why could they not visit it and see what it looked like?

Fate can be a bitch sometimes, and it was fate that ordained that Estelle should walk into the café at that moment, looking drawn and unhappy.

"Bon soir, mes soeurs," she greeted them, although there were some there that objected to being referred to as 'sister' by the woman who had cuckolded her husband.

"Has anyone seen Jacques? I have been to the house, but he is not there, and I cannot reach him on his mobile." There was silence for a moment, then the formidable Claudine Frambois sniffed loudly and exclaimed, "But why should he be at home, when his wife ran away to Monaco?"

Estelle burst into tears, and dropped into a vacant chair.

She snivelled, blew her nose, and then told her story. "My lover, the British yacht broker, has found a young stewardess from one of the yachts, and has told me to go back to my husband, I don't know what to do, but I need to see and speak to Jacques. Do you think he will take me back?"

The women around the table all looked at each other in embarrassment, then Sandrine Bellat put her arm around Estelle and hugged her close. "Chérie, you were wrong to have treated Jacques so badly, he is a good man, but if you can find him tonight, maybe you can persuade him to give you another chance." She dried Estelle's eyes and ordered a round of 'Kirs' for them all to drink.

***

At Club 202, there were only the founder members left downstairs. The girls had ganged together, and had taken Jacques by the hands and led him uncomplainingly up the stairs to one of the bedrooms.

The four men and Catherine sat at the table and sipped their coffees and Armagnacs. The music still played quietly in the background, and Patrick stroked the back of Catherine's hand as he summed up the evening for them all.

"What a triumph, mes amis! What a night to remember for all of us! Commandant Lebel will be a new man tomorrow, no more sadness at the departure of Estelle, no more growling at his gendarmes, and a night to go into the annals of Club 202. Let us toast to ourselves, to pleasure and to the Club!"

They all clinked their glasses and chuckled happily.

From upstairs there came a bull-like bellow, and Christophe grinned, "Ah! The Commandant is opening his presents."

Patrick and Catherine said their 'goodnights' and, climbing the stairs, headed for the largest bedroom and opened the door. There was a sleepy challenge from the bed, and Patrick discerned bodies wrapped in the duvet.

"What is going on?" he demanded, "Who is in here?" One of the dancers' young voices answered him, "Gaëlle said that just she and one other would stay with the Commandant, so we picked Chantalle. We four are sleeping here."

"Bonne nuit, mes petites, sleep well," said Patrick, as he quietly closed the door. He and Catherine found one of the other bedrooms, and quickly slid under the duvet.

Christophe, Jean-Michel and Gilbert sat quietly in the smoking room. Gilbert went to the bar and fetched the bottle of Armagnac and topped up their glasses, while Christophe put another log on the fire.

"Mes amis," he began, "I too would like a birthday party to remember sometime, will you agree to the same sort of party for me?" The other two laughed and said that they saw no reason not to afford their friend the same pleasure.

The three of them decided that it would be unwise to drive home, considering the amount that they had drunk, and as there was a total of five bedrooms, they should each take one for the night. They also agreed that it would be easier to cope with their spouses' ire in the cold light of day.

***

Back in Puget-Théniers the group of wives had now dropped to only four; they were finishing their drinks prior to driving Estelle in search of her husband. Claudine, Sandrine and Auditte, who was Gilbert's wife, were all sitting with Estelle. They had been discussing how good a friend Patrick Paysan was to their husbands, and what a selfless husband he was, allowing his wife to go and stay with her sister for so long.

***

Gilbert was the first to leave the smoking room, he bid his friends goodnight and mounted the stairs. The first room that he tried was occupied, and by the light from the landing, he saw the Commandant's arm handcuffed to the bed head, and two smaller figures cuddled up to him. He smiled as he closed the door, shaking his head in admiration and more than a little envy. He used one of the bathrooms, rubbing his teeth with his forefinger and some toothpaste that was there.

The next room that he tried was empty, and he quickly stripped off and slipped under the covers. He was about to switch out the bedside light when Christophe stuck his head in through the doorway. "Gilbert," he whispered, "can I share your bed? Jean-Michel has taken the other room, and there are 4 girls in the last bedroom." Gilbert was not concerned about sharing the bed with Christophe—neither of them was exceptionally large—and they were old friends, having done their army service together. "OK," he grumbled, "but no snoring, or you can go and share with Jean-Michel."

The house became nearly silent, no more bellows from the commandant, vague murmurings from the girls' room, and only the sound of heavy breathing from Patrick.

***

On the road from Puget-Théniers, the old Land Rover Discovery belonging to Sandrine Bellat was spinning along, covering the fifteen kilometres at the legal speed limit. The four women had decided that the obvious place to search for Jacques was the Club 202, and it gave them a wonderful reason to surprise their husbands and see the inside of the house, which only Estelle had seen before.

"Jean-Michel will die of embarrassment when I march in on him – I cannot wait!" chortled Claudine, "he has warned me to never come looking for him there."

***

In the bedroom used by the four girls, there was some discomfort. A queen-sized bed can feel small for four girls, even girls as svelte and

35

slim as these were. So Candice, a long-legged beauty with tumbling masses of raven black hair, decided to try and find more comfortable quarters. She wrapped a towel around her naked body and crept onto the landing. She knew that Jacques was in the end bedroom with Gaëlle and Chantalle, so she tried the room next to the one she had left. There was the sound of someone breathing deeply in their sleep, and she was able to see that it was just one man, sleeping right on the edge of the huge bed. Carefully Candice slipped under the duvet, dropping her towel on the floor.

Jean-Michel, used to being forced by Claudine to sleep right over on the edge of the bed, was fast asleep, the pastis, wine and Armagnac making him insensible to sound or movement. Within seconds Candice was asleep; even asleep she felt a little cold, so unconsciously she wriggled across the bed, wrapping herself around the warm body of Jean-Michel.

***

Sandrine idled the Discovery into the parking area behind Club 202, and the four women got out of the car quietly. There were no lights on at the house, but there were a number of vehicles parked. Sandrine recognized her husband's car, that belonging to Patrick, and the police car used by Jacques. The expensive mini-van with the slogan 'ENTERTAINMENT AT HOME' on the side was not known to any of the women.

Without speaking, but with feelings of unease, the four wives moved towards the front door.

People in the country often do not bother locking their doors at night, so there was no surprise when the door was found to be unlocked. Auditte scrabbled for a light switch, and the hallway became visible. The four crept forward into the main room, and turned on the lights there as well.

The long table was set, still covered with platters of half-eaten snacks. There were empty glasses and bottles scattered around on the bar, windowsills, mantelpiece and table. Flung over the backs of a couple of chairs, there were brassieres covered in sequins. Claudine picked up a feather fan from the floor and looked at the other women.

"I am going to cut Jean-Michel's balls off," she muttered with quiet venom.

Sandrine was already heading for the stairs, and the others crowded after her.

The women arrived at the door of the first bedroom at the top of the stairs. Sandrine swung the door open and switched on the light. She was extremely surprised to see her husband sharing a bed with Gilbert. Auditte was right behind her and rushed into the room, screaming at Gilbert, "Sale pédé, dirty homosexual, how could you, with another man you filthy brute, what am I going to tell our children?"

The two friends sat up in bed, trying desperately to work out where they were, what was happening, and why. Sandrine swung a fist at Christophe, connecting with a solid thump, and he collapsed back onto his pillows. Auditte jumped on top of Gilbert, striking him around the face with both hands while he vainly tried to protect himself.

In the meantime, Claudine had crashed open the door opposite, where, in the glare of the light, she saw a girl of extraordinary beauty snuggled up to her husband's naked back. With a shrill shriek of rage, she flung herself onto the bed and went for poor Candice like a tigress. The young dancer had reflexes like a cat, and managed to slide out from under the attack, so Claudine changed direction, and started beating the pulp out of Jean-Michel. He woke with a start, saw Claudine swinging at him and immediately screamed, "Please, I was on my side! Don't hit me!"

Estelle rushed into the next bedroom, and was amazed to see Patrick Paysan and an attractive dark-haired woman clutching each other in terror, having been woken by the uproar. She left them there

37

and threw herself at the next door, where she stood and stared, one hand still on the light switch, while Candice pushed past her and jumped into the bed with three other girls, all of whom looked terrified.

Shaking her head in bemusement, she turned to the door at the end of the passage, opened it and switched on the light. She let out a wail and staggered back holding her hands to her breast. There, in all his glory was her 'boring' husband, handcuffed to the bed. He was holding with his free arm, in a gesture of protection, two incredibly beautiful girls. Estelle sank slowly to the floor, sobbing quietly while Jacques, in unbearable embarrassment, softly said, "Gaëlle chérie, do you think you could unlock my cuffs? This is my wife Estelle, who has turned up unexpectedly." Without a word Gaëlle started to search the bed for the keys, which she found eventually. She unlocked the cuffs and slithered over to hug Chantalle, while Jacques slid out of the bed and wrapped a towel around his waist.

Down the corridor, there was an abating of the screams and yells, as hurried and desperate explanations were garbled by terrified husbands to incensed wives.

Claudine barged into the room where the four terrified dancers were crouching under the duvet. She singled out Candice and said to her, in a voice resembling a snake's, "Listen to me you little whore, my husband swears that he did not even know that you were in the bed. Is this true? Be careful how you answer, because I am ready to make you much less attractive!"

Candice, who was crying quietly shook her head, "There was no room for me here, and I just climbed into the bed with him. I tried not to even touch him, but I was cold, so I guess I just moved over to him, but I promise that he never woke up. Please Madame, I'm not a bad girl, don't hurt me I beg you." The fight went out of Claudine straight away, and she turned around and left the bedroom. She shook her head when she saw Jacques Lebel sitting on the floor of the corridor and cuddling his sobbing wife Estelle, but decided to try and sort out one problem at a time.

Sandrine and Auditte were sitting on their husbands' bed, both trying to tend to the wounds that they had inflicted, while Christophe and Gilbert both let out moans of pain. Sandrine looked at Auditte and started laughing, "Do you honestly think our idiot husbands could ever be 'gays', we are the most stupid women in the world, and I suspect that this is going to cost us plenty!"

Claudine put an arm around Jean-Michel and held him close. "Chéri, I am sorry that I suspected the worst, but you must know what it looked like, and she was so beautiful." Her husband just looked at her and smiled.

An hour later the fire in the smoking room was crackling, Catherine was busy making coffee in the kitchen, and the whole unlikely company were trying to avoid each others' eyes.

Patrick was wearing a dashing silk dressing gown, with a cravat around his neck. He looked at the assembled company, the bevy of beauties cuddled together on the big settee; Jacques and Estelle Lebel, who were sharing a big armchair, stroking each other's faces in disbelief; while Christophe and Sandrine, Gilbert and Auditte, Jean-Michel and Claudine all sat at the table holding hands.

"Eh bien mes enfants!" he began, "This has been a night of great surprises and confusion. I suggest we all go to our respective homes and remember never to tell the story to anyone outside this group. Do you all agree?" Everyone looked around, catching the glances of all the others, then they all, almost in unison, nodded.

***

In the following days there were all sorts of rumours heard. Jean-Michel, Gilbert and Christophe all bore bruises and other signs of assault and battery, yet they stuck to their story that they had had a disagreement whist in their cups and had beaten each other;

meanwhile their three wives became extremely caring and gentle with their husbands.

Jacques Lebel became a smiling and easy-going commandant at work, hurrying home as soon as he could at the end of each day. Estelle was a changed woman, caring and undemanding. She had a new friend who came to visit sometimes…the friend's name was Gaëlle.

And Patrick and Catherine? Patrick's wife wrote and said that she no longer wished to live with Patrick, so he settled a reasonable pension on her, and most weekends Catherine would come and stay with him.

Patrick found a legal loophole in the lease that the founder members of Club 202 had signed, so the furniture was sold, the house was closed up again, and that was the end of Club 202…a sorry demise to an exciting chapter in the life of Puget-Théniers.

January 2012

Cold in Puget

Puget-Théniers gets cold in the winter. Where I live, in a small secluded valley, it gets colder still, thanks to the surrounding hills that block out the sun from the start of December to halfway through January. When I say cold, I mean nights that register -12°C, and days where the temperature never gets above freezing.

In order to drive to the village, I have to start my Jeep a good fifteen minutes before I want to leave. I also have to stoke up the fire and lay in enough logs each morning.

Having lived for many years in the tropics, I habitually wear a sarong instead of pyjamas, and I have a colourful selection that I wear with some panache (at least for a sixty-four-year-old). A combination of machismo and stupidity has always driven me to a stoic habit in the early mornings: I clear the old ash out of the fireplace, and carry it out to the ash heap at the end of the patio wearing nothing but my sarong, and with bare feet. For years I was convinced that this first breath of freezing air, with my feet either sticking to the icy slates, or else up to my bare ankles in snow, was good for me and helped accelerate the circulation of blood round my near-naked body.

Wrong.

This year I caught the most horrendous cold. I woke up in my unheated bedroom with ice on the blanket and rime all over the open window. I could not breathe, I sneezed about fifteen times consecutively and I felt like death. Dragging myself downstairs to the warmth of the sitting room, I switched on the television to catch the early morning news. I was confronted with a sports report on the ODI cricket match being played between South Africa and India; the match was in Cape Town, and the scenes of Newlands in the sunshine almost had me in tears. I felt even colder.

41

I dosed myself with everything in the medical cabinet, had a spiced hot wine with my lunch, and slothed around the house keeping warm and sniffling.

That evening I decided to stay a bit warmer, so I put a hot water bottle in my bed (what a wuss!), closed the bedroom window, and dressed differently for bed.

Gone were the élan and the panache.

I ended up wearing my grey and yellow sarong, topped by a heavy black T-shirt, set off by blue woollen socks. I finished off the ensemble with a green Springbok beanie.

It struck me that I was truly a bizarre figure, deserving of some derision. In fact the wildcat, who was sitting on the windowsill, bared his fangs at me before disappearing into the darkness – I am sure that he was laughing at me.

The night was terrible. The T-shirt tried to strangle me as I rolled over (it seems that I was able to turn inside it, a bit like a honey-badger turns inside its skin). The beanie moved down over my eyes, and I thought I had gone blind, while my feet started to sweat in the woollen socks.

Morning brought no relief, so I staggered out of bed and headed downstairs. Now, my stairs are wooden, steep and very slippery. Socks should never be worn while negotiating them. I ended up in a bruised and mewling heap at the bottom, nothing broken, but sore and utterly lacking in dignity.

I followed my usual routine, and cleared the fireplace, but decided to cover my feet before venturing outside, so I donned a pair of favourite sea-boots.

I was just emptying the ash bucket when a voice startled me. My neighbour, Gilbert, was standing on the patio staring at me as though I was a demented and dangerous madman. He rolled his eyes at my dashing sarong, the sea-boots and the beanie pulled over my ears and, indicating my outlandish outfit, timidly asked whether I was going to a fancy-dress lunch. I tried to explain, between sniffs and sneezes, but

I felt that he did not believe me, and was convinced that he had surprised me in the midst of a rather unhealthy perversion.

A few days later, when I had recovered and was sure that I was not about to expire from double pneumonia, I ventured down to the village for supplies. Having stocked up on essentials (wine, bread, cheese etc.), I wandered into the local bar for a 'petit rouge'.

Philu, who owns the bar, and Sandrine, his beautiful barista, stared at me, and had a whispered conversation while Sandrine poured my wine. She brought it to me, smiled a knowing smile and asked me why I was not wearing my 'jolis vêtements' – my pretty clothes.

I was aghast and appalled: thanks to Gilbert, the whole village now thinks that I dress in slightly feminine clothing and perform perverse sexual acts on my own!

It will take years for me to convince the local population that I may be eccentric, but not a deviant ... although it could be fun to play along....

January 2013

The Culinary Dangers of France

Whilst watching television a couple of nights ago, I was startled by the sound of someone hammering on the shutters. I leapt up, opened the door, and swung out the shutters. Having already switched on the outside lights, I saw that there were two gentlemen in the uniform of the 'pompiers', the firemen of France. I invited them in and settled them down with a glass of wine, while I wrote out a cheque for the pompiers' Christmas collection.

(Two things strike me immediately—back in South Africa, *no one* would just open their doors at nine o'clock at night, and no one even knows what a cheque book is anymore. *Plus ça change…*)

One of the young men regaled me with stories of his exploits as a boy, when he used to gather wild mushrooms from the land that I own. In those days the house was almost a ruin, and I had only bought it, restored it and started living there some fourteen years before.

His stories brought to mind an event from about five years ago. The owner of the bar in Puget-Théniers was a fast talking local by the name of Philippe, usually shortened to Philu. He was an engaging character, full of bombast and bravura, a definite favourite with the local ladies around the age of thirty, both married and single. He asked me one day whether he could come onto my property and collect mushrooms, and I happily agreed.

As usual, I was about to depart on a trip somewhere, so when I visited the bar in late November to say my farewells, I reminded Philu that I would expect him to dry some mushrooms for me. He grinned and told me not to worry (which should have immediately set my 'this-could-be-trouble' antennae quivering), and away I went.

Now the locals are inclined to gently pull the legs of any 'foreigner' (anyone who was not born within fifteen kilometres of Puget-Théniers), and tell them that all sorts of local flora and fauna are not just edible, but delicious. I have been told to eat the small 'loirs',

44

rodents that infest my roof during the summer. I have never tried eating them (although I have been tempted to skin them and make a very fetching waistcoat from the pelts!), and I have never gathered wild mushrooms, as I couldn't be sure of what I was putting in my mouth. I am a seaman, not a farmer.

I returned to Puget after a couple of months, settled back into my home, and eventually stopped into the bar on a bright but cold February day. Philu seemed overjoyed to see me, poured me a 'grand rouge', and happily gave me a little tin—the kind that one used to buy peanuts in—with a removable plastic lid. He explained that he had dried the mushrooms carefully, and that they would keep for ages. All I had to do was to soak them in water for an hour or two, dry them, then chop them up and use them as I would normal store- bought mushrooms.

A few weeks went by and one morning I woke up with a yen for a mushroom omelette. No mushrooms in the fridge, but then I remembered the little tin of dried wild mushrooms. I followed Philu's instructions, and by about eleven there was the delicious smell of mushrooms sautéing in butter. I folded them into a three-egg omelette and settled down to a proper breakfast feast. The mushrooms were truly delicious, and I savoured every last mouthful. Full, replete (and all those other adjectives to describe having overeaten on wonderful food), I washed the dishes and turned on the television to watch some rugby.

After about 30 minutes, I began to feel a little nauseous. After an hour I was *very* nauseous, also sweating and shaky.

I eventually retired to my bedroom, opened the window wide, and climbed into bed. I lay there, my stomach in knots, and tried to go to sleep.

I really wish that I hadn't.

I woke up screaming, the memory of a terrible dream still burning behind my eyes … only to see the dream now on my wall: a lizard of at least two metres in length, stuck to my wall. It was tasting the air

45

with its loathsome tongue, and seemed to be staring at me hungrily. I blinked, but it didn't go away, so I got out of bed and made my way to the upstairs bathroom.

There was another lizard there, but this one had teeth and seemed to be thinking about which part of me it was going to chew off first. I was now fully awake, and as the multi-toothed lizard faded away, I realized that I was having some serious hallucinations. I drank a couple of glasses of water and went back to bed. Over the next twenty-four hours I was as sick as a dog, and had all sorts of terrifying dreams and hallucinations.

Finally, I drifted into an exhausted sleep, and woke up feeling drained but back in control.

It was another day before I found the strength to make my way down to the village. Philu was most unimpressed with my complaint that he had poisoned me, saying that I was lucky that he had left a couple of 'special' mushrooms in the tin—other people had to pay to find them!

After that experience, I certainly won't be paying anyone for 'special' mushrooms, and am slightly paranoid about accepting mushrooms of any description from anybody.

December 2016

Smoked Hams

With the relentless advance of age—and the equally relentless and disturbing diminishment of income—I have been thinking of ways to pad out my wallet during retirement.

It is all very well to hope that there is enough saved money in the 'kitty' to last one through until death, but when, as in my case, there is no index-linked pension from a government agency or an international corporation, one can become a trifle paranoid about how long the 'moolah' is going to last.

It really is most inconvenient that we are not issued with a ticket or a slip of paper giving us our 'check-out' date and time, as that would make advance planning so much easier.

The thought of approaching a very ripe old age and knowing that there is only indigence and starvation to look forward to is pretty harrowing. Almost as bad would be to realize, as one shuffles off one's mortal coil, that there is enough cash in the bank to party like a hooligan for a couple of years, but time has run out early.

Decisions, decisions.

The only real answer is to make sure that there is a big enough reserve of 'lolly' with which to party like hell whenever one wants to, in the absolute certainty that there will be plenty to fall back on in one's dotage. Not easy. When working in a regular job, a certain amount can be saved. This obviously depends on the care with which one's partner or spouse manages the cheque book, the number of iPhones or thoroughbred ponies the offspring desperately need, and one's own decidedly wild tastes in cars, whisky, travel and partners.

In my case life is a little simpler. Three ex-spouses have made a bit of difference to the present lifestyle, but not huge. I have no parasitic little bundles of joy that can empty my wallet in a heartbeat, develop a taste for caviar at the age of two, or bully me into buying them a Porsche at the age of eighteen. My own needs are fairly monastic, in that I am happy to drink good red wines that do not cost and arm or a leg; to eat lentils and rice with boring regularity; to coax my aging Jeep into running for another year, then another, ad infinitum; and to travel economy class despite the discomfort, the ghastly products labelled as 'airline food', and the risk of contracting loathsome viruses from loathsome people.

Despite this very simple and meagre lifestyle, I have decided to try and earn a little more cash by utilizing the land on which my house is built.

I have around twenty-four acres of land, of which four or so are arable. There are a number of oak trees on the property, which are supposed to nurture the growth of truffles, and a few hazelnut trees which are meant to do the same.

I have had one miniscule truffle in twelve years. This is not a success story.

I need a crop that can be easily planted, produced, harvested and sold.

The answer, very simply, is Mary Jane.

(For those of you who are not aficionados of the modern lexicon of drug names, MJ is the pseudonym of marijuana, also known as 'weed', 'dagga', 'leaf', 'pot', 'skunk', 'burrito', and many more imaginative and harmless sounding names.)

I have unlimited clean water from the stream at the bottom of my property, and I have room for a couple of long plastic tunnels, in which I would be able to grow copious quantities of hydroponically enriched 'ganga'. This would, I feel sure, guarantee a very comfortable retirement, without the need to leave the little bit of paradise that I call home.

The only drawback is the intractability of the French government, which—at present anyway—doesn't seem interested in legalizing the use of cannabis, even for medicinal purposes.

But I have a plan.

Living on my land, and one of the reasons that I have had so few truffles in past years, is a plethora of wild pigs. These beasts root around happily, and eat just about anything that my land produces. So, why not introduce the wild pigs to marijuana? Letting them eat it would surely turn their meat into a truly different gastronomic experience. I don't anticipate that high hogs would cause any problems ... although ... hmm ... what if they have a bad reaction and turn paranoid? That could be entertaining but probably not very safe. On the other hand, I could simply have legs of wild boar slow-smoked over smoldering bunches of the weed. How could the French government, so proud of its culinary history, turn down a world first?

'SKUNK SMOKED HAM, Get High on Jambon!' It could be exported to Spain: 'CERDO SALVAJE NARCOTICO, Alto en Jamón!'

People would flock to Puget-Théniers to buy the ham that makes their mother-in-law so sweet to be with, after just one sandwich. With a little imagination, I can see the local restaurants producing a 'daube de sanglier' (wild boar stew), adding in some of the famous magic mushrooms that grow in the area, and advertising it as 'Daube Demente', or Madness Stew. The possibilities are endless, and the prospects very exciting.

I feel sure that Melton Mowbray would contact me, asking whether they could use the hams in their pork pies—'Pot Pork Pies'—would sell faster than ordinary ones. The whole idea of bacon and eggs in the morning would change, pork sausages on the barbeque would become a cerebral pleasure, as opposed to simply a gastronomic one.

I feel that I am on the threshold of true wealth! If I can just stay out of jail

Jan 2018

49

Dangerous Driving in Puget

In Puget-Théniers we have a small supermarket, a Carrefour Market, where one can purchase most of the necessities of life—wine, cheese, bread and a host of stuff that is sometimes a surprise to find in a small rural village of only fifteen-hundred residents. I was once amazed to see a large and elderly lady with a trolley full of produce, topped off with a set of huge lacy underwear in a lurid pinky-orange colour. She became impatient at the check- out, where another old bat was regaling the cashier with stories of her grandchildren. The purchaser of the underwear loudly suggested that the grandmother should pay and move, at which point war was declared, and the aforesaid grandmother hissed, "Et toi, avec ton 'slip' de pute!" Roughly translated this means: "And you, with your whore's knickers!"

The ensuing battle of words brought the *real* parentage of the offspring of both women into question, and the morals of both antagonists were discussed with some venom. Eventually a manageress was called to restore order, and I swear that there was a sigh of disappointment from the entranced shoppers waiting in the cashiers' queues.

The reader may have gathered that Puget has a high percentage of elderly inhabitants, and the proof of this is that yearly, one sees more gaps in the line of old codgers at the bar, and bare spaces on the park benches where old women gather to discuss the more scandalous goings-on in the village. I suspect that the places on the benches are 'held', and that it sometimes takes a few days for the news to be digested that another pensioner has shuffled off their mortal coil. An uninformed tourist would be rudely moved on if they were brash enough to sit down in one of these spaces to enjoy the peace and quiet.

The Carrefour Market has a vaguely adequate parking area behind the store, and a set of self-service petrol pumps in the front, so all vehicles have to leave the parking by passing through the service station area. The other day I was involved in a 'contre-temps' that I suspect occurs quite regularly, considering the large number of 'wrinklies' and other versions of senior citizens.

I had finished shopping and had packed the bags in the back of my Jeep, when I saw an aged fellow carefully climbing into his Renault Mégane, while his equally decrepit wife dropped their shopping bags into the boot. He started the car, and the reversing lights came on, while Madame slowly closed the boot and stood clear. I started the Jeep, and held position, as it looked as though the old boy was going to take his time in backing out of his parking space. His wife now stood behind the car, and a little to one side, waving her hand impatiently, and shouting at the top of her voice, "Vas-y, vas-y, vas-y!", literally, "Come on!" or "Go, go!" At this point things started to go wrong, when an ancient acquaintance of Madame's struggled past, and stopped for a word or ten, as old people are prone to do. Madame stopped shouting to her husband (who probably couldn't hear her anyway), but neglected to stop waving her hand, so the old fellow carried on reversing.

Straight into the headlights of the Peugeot parked behind him.

Madame at this point shrieked, "Merde! Idiot!" The other old woman hobbled off as rapidly as she could, and Monsieur struggled out of the driver's side, shouting at his wife. I believe that I heard the word "crétine" used a couple of times, which certainly seemed to excite the old lady further. They both inspected the damage to the two vehicles, which was minimal: a scratch on the Peugeot, and a broken tail-light on the Renault. Still exchanging words not usually used by a loving couple, the old man climbed back into the car, while Madame opened the passenger door and slowly started to lower herself onto the seat.

At which point the old man drove off.

Madame tumbled to the tarmac, screaming obscenities at her spouse, while he slammed on the brakes and again struggled out of the car. Madame seemed to be totally unhurt, and managed to get to her feet by using the stationary car for support, but her pride was certainly badly damaged, and she let her husband have it with both barrels. From what I could gather, she brought up the subject that her mother had warned her about marrying beneath her station, and that it was a surprise that their numerous children had not turned out to be imbeciles like their father.

They breed them tough in Puget-Théniers, and quite quickly the old couple got back in the car and drove off—possibly they wished to avoid the owner of the Peugeot. I pulled out after them, and we all headed for the exit. Unfortunately, there was a car waiting to use the petrol pump, so the old guy stopped to wait, and I had to as well. A couple of other cars pulled up behind me, and we all sat and stewed in the heat.

Madame, realizing that this could take some time, got out of the Renault, and opened the boot, apparently to pack some of her purchases in a 'cool' bag for frozen items. It so happened that one of the cars behind me chose this moment to honk the horn in a show of Gallic impatience. Madame turned and gave me a virulent look, which I swear made me break into a muck sweat, and I unconsciously locked all the doors. In turning, the old witch left a couple of frozen boxes precariously on the edge of the boot, so as the old man jerked the Renault forward when the blocking car moved, the boxes fell to the ground.

Madame again gave vent to her temper, but I felt that this time, through no fault of my own, I shared the outpouring of rage and hate with her husband. She picked up her boxes and followed the Renault into the refueling area, and I was able to slip past without any hideous confrontation.

I am very glad that I didn't have to spend the evening in their house, as I suspect the recriminations would have gone on for a very long time.

July 2018

French Resistance Party
Saint-Joseph, 1961

Monsieur Claude Berger was forty-seven years old. He was a local builder, taking on small renovations and projects in the area. He usually worked alone, only occasionally needing a hand to help him. He often thought back wistfully to 1940, when he had joined the resistance movement. He had loved the glamour, the intrigue, the danger and the excitement. When one is twenty-six years old, danger is often the spice of life.

Berger was happily married to Odile and they had two children, a boy of twelve and a girl of fourteen. One of the highlights of Claude's year was the Resistance supper, held in July and attended by all the surviving members of the local group. There were eight of them still living in the area, and this was almost the only date that they all got together and reminisced over the days when they were young, agile and being hunted by the hated Boche. Claude was a gentle man who worshiped his wife and adored his children, but became belligerent and stubborn when he imbibed too much wine.

The most vociferous and bossy member of the group was Odile's elder sister, Corinne, a twice-married and extremely pretty lady, who had for a short period been Claude Berger's lover. They had been young, cold, and hiding in a barn while the German troops combed the surrounding farms looking for them. Circumstances and opportunity led to their frantic and passionate lovemaking amongst the bales of hay, a diversion that they repeated as frequently as they could within acceptable boundaries for the next six months.

The relationship ended with the arrival of a young Free French officer, sent to bring a new radio prior to the Allied invasion. Corinne took one look at Lieutenant Debussy and almost passed out with immediate desire and adoration.

Claude and Corinne remained friendly and were able to carry on working together without any animosity, even when Corinne and the dashing Lieutenant were married by the local priest. Debussy travelled north towards Paris a few weeks after the wedding, and was killed in a German air strike on the road.

Corinne stayed with the group, fighting on to the day of Liberation, when she packed her bags and headed for Normandy to find Lieutenant Debussy's family. Find them she did, and she stayed with them in their village for nearly two years before falling in love with another soldier returned from the war. She bore her husband a daughter and named her Anna, but the marriage did not last, and Corinne arrived back in Saint-Joseph with her daughter in 1951.

The other members of the group were Justin, the local gendarme; Serge, a forester and a supplier of firewood; the twin brothers Gilbert and Daniel who ran the village 'tabac'; and the old Marquis de Lent, who had been the leader of the group. Dearly loved and respected, this gentleman was now eighty years old and a widower, cared for by his only daughter.

The supper always took place in the early evening, on a grassy bank close to the small river, where there were tree stumps to sit on and a wide sward of soft grass to set up the trestle tables. By tradition the dinner started with the eight veteran fighters catching a few trout in the river, usually using worms as bait. These fish were then gutted and grilled on a small fire while bottles of wine and cider were quaffed.

The fish were eaten with loaves of bread, using the fingers with much blowing on the hot flakes of white flesh, just as the group had so often done during the war. There would then be a period of quiet reminiscence—shared memories of friends killed in action and others who had passed on later of old age or sickness. Many toasts were drunk to departed comrades, to the leaders of the Free French, to Winston Churchill. Everyone became a little lachrymose, until the old Marquis would finally bang the table and exhort them with a hearty

"Alors mes braves! Enough of this, let us enjoy our lives and the joy of our loved ones!"

One of the band would now climb up the small knoll close by, and wave towards the church spire where one of the villagers had been keeping watch. Shortly thereafter the sound of children's excited voices grew closer as the villagers arrived, laden with baskets of food, more wine, and a few musical instruments. There were the families of the resistance group, the children often wearing their parents' war decorations (as the display of medals was eschewed by the group themselves). The priest was there carrying a piano accordion, the young schoolteacher had control of the school choir, and there were visitors, invited by the villagers to this special occasion.

There was only enough space at the tables for about twenty people to sit, so the other forty or so spread rugs on the ground or found tree stumps to sit on. The evening was warm, with not a cloud in the sky, and as the sun dipped behind the knoll, stars started to appear. Paraffin lamps were lit for the table, and others were wedged around the grounds.

The children chased each other around in the shadows, and the teenage boys postured and posed, trying to attract the girls' attention. The adults' voices grew louder as wine bottles were emptied, and there were bursts of hilarity as risqué stories were recounted. The priest started to play his accordion softly, someone joined in on a guitar, gently brushing the chords as the melody was recognized. The schoolteacher corralled some of the children, who started to sing one of the old local favourites in their pure and sweet voices. Conversation quietened and then ceased as the adults hummed along or tapped the table to keep time.

The songs were local, some a little sad, some lively and invigorating, and after about an hour the guitar player called for a break, "My fingers are almost bleeding, and only wine can cure them!" he cried.

Conversation resumed as people got up, moved around, spoke to friends and greeted strangers.

Blanche, the daughter of the Marquis, had brought with her a tall, distinguished-looking man-friend. He was sparely built with short grey hair, wearing a green jacket that was certainly not cut in France. They made a handsome couple as they moved around towards the table, where Blanche poured them each a beaker of wine. Claude had been staring at the man in the green jacket for a while, unnoticed by the rest of the company.

"Still today I spit on the Boche, filthy vermin!" Claude said to the bar-keeping twins next to him. "I want none of them, ever, near to this village," he continued, still staring at Blanche's companion. Odile took his arm, trying to calm his obvious antagonism, but he shook her hand off.

"Blanche," he called, too loudly for the short distance between them, "come and introduce your friend!"

The Marquis tried to rise from his bench, but Blanche gently pushed his shoulder down, keeping him in his seat. She took the tall man's hand and moved down the table towards Claude. The tall man moved in front of Blanche, smiled and offered his right hand to Claude, "Erich Schwinger, very pleased to meet you," he said in accented but good French.

Claude rose from the bench, leaned on the table and spat on the man's hand. "Go back to the shit-pile that you live in, you are not welcome here," he shouted. "Where were you in 1944, you murdering bastard?" Claude continued, shaking with rage.

The crowd was silent, only the Marquis and Blanche seemed to be trying to say something to Claude.

Erich took a handkerchief from his pocket and wiped the saliva from his hand; he smiled at Claude, slipped the jacket from his shoulders, and presented his left forearm for Claude's inspection.

Claude looked down and his eyes fixed a tattoo on Erich's arm: the letter 'A' followed by six figures …

There was absolute silence, while Claude gripped the edge of the table with both hands and closed his eyes. Tears appeared on his cheeks, squeezing out from between his eyelids.

Eventually Claude spoke. "Please forgive me, I had no right to presuppose, I would do anything to take back my words."

Erich patted him on the shoulder, "There is nothing to forgive," he said.

The Marquis rose at the head of the table, "Venez, mes braves! Music, wine, laughter—we must have them all!"

And the party continued.

April 2012

Politics in Puget-Théniers

Last weekend was the time for local elections in France, and everything became a lot more heated than I expected. Last year our incumbent mayor, Monsieur Velay, was so certain of his victory that he laid on a case of champagne to celebrate. Unfortunately for him the result was so close that there was a recount, and the champagne had to be cooled again two days later. I am used to dirty politics—after all I am from Africa, where there is no other brand—but I was astounded and appalled by the savagery displayed by the local politicians of the Alpes-Maritimes.

I was going about my shopping on the Saturday morning and looking forward to having a beer at the café, when I was accosted by Monsieur Velay. He grabbed my arm and fixed me with a feverish eye. "Do you vote?" he asked, rather as though voting was a slightly risqué deviation. I explained that I was not registered as a French resident, and that I was pretty sure that this precluded me from voting in France. Monsieur Velay didn't let go of my arm. "I'm sure that you are allowed to; please, Monsieur Beadon, go to the voting station tomorrow and ask," he croaked with a look of desperation on his face.

Now M. Velay is about as far 'right' as a politician can go without growing a small moustache and goose-stepping, so I was interested to see who his nearest rival was for the position of mayor. It turned out to be an absolute crazy by the name of Jules Penard who represented the National Front. Why Jules has not grown the small moustache I really do not know, because he makes Attila the Hun seem a milk-sop liberal by comparison, and his party, the National Front, would certainly throw all foreigners out of France as quickly as possible, given the chance.

I was told about Jules Penard by the bunch of wrinkly grey-hairs who support the bar at lunchtime most days. For once they were not glassy eyed with lust while watching Coline the barmaid's every move; they were in deep and serious conversation while darting dark glances towards the other end of the bar. The target of their malevolent stares was Spike. Spike is the local tattooist and caricaturist, and is a man of exceptional talent. He tattoos freehand, and film stars have been known to fly in from Los Angeles to have Spike embellish their skin with one of his original and unique designs.

It took me a while to understand what had been going on, and it was only when the incomparable Sandrine, the senior barista, walked past me in tears that I was able to piece together what had transpired in the dark and dirty world of Puget Politics.

It was no great hardship to put an arm around Sandrine and ask her why she was crying. She immediately sobbed out that 'someone'—and at this point she threw Spike a filthy look—had drawn a terribly suggestive portrait of her father. Sandrine is the only (and incredibly nubile) daughter of M. Velay. I enquired as delicately as I could where this portrait was. Sandrine told me that there were copies of the hideous drawing all over the town. I took myself off to tour the streets of Puget, and sure enough, there were foolscap-sized drawings everywhere. They showed M. Velay in a very bad light. He was not known to be allied to Madame Le Pen's party, but Spike had drawn him naked, wearing a spiky dog collar, crouched and chained to a table leg. Above him, an equally naked (except for thigh high boots) Madame Le Pen wielded a whip. The drawing was undoubtedly of M. Velay and Madame Le Pen, and both had grimaces of intense enjoyment on their faces. M. Velay's genitals were depicted in miniscule fashion, and his tongue lolled out of the side of his mouth in a disgusting manner. I could see why Sandrine was so upset.

On returning to the bar I saw that the crowd had surrounded Spike, and that he was being heckled and shouted down each time he tried to speak. It seemed that Spike had no political leanings, but that he had been approached by the National Front to draw M. Velay in an unattractive and ludicrous pose for a hefty fee. The crowd was telling him that it was unfair to make M. Velay an object of scorn while leaving M. Penard alone. After a while, Spike nodded, gave a small smile, and headed up the side street to his tattoo parlour. In less than thirty minutes, he reappeared with a stack of A4 flyers under his arm, and he strode off across the bridge in the direction of the post office. I followed and begged a copy off him.

It was a masterpiece. M. Penard was depicted wearing a type of leather suit commonly seen during gay pride rallies. The bottom had been cut out, and the arms were left bare. He was standing with his legs braced straight, bent over at the hips with his abundantly hairy bum cocked at a very feminine angle, and looking over his shoulder with a revoltingly obscene smirk on his face. Madame Le Pen was again in the picture, still naked and be-whipped, though this time her face was decidedly vicious.

Spike stuck one of the new batch of drawings alongside each of the earlier works of art, and justice was done.

God bless politics in Puget-Théniers.

July 2013

Burglar Alarms

I had just come back from a particularly harrowing yacht delivery. The boat should have remained in someone's bath as a toy, the weather was horrendous, and the legal machinations were exhausting.

I arrived at my house in Puget-Théniers to find it covered in snow, but warm and snug thanks to Anita, a lady from the village, who had lit a fire and turned on the towel warmers in the bathrooms.

I made a simple supper, enjoyed a glass of wine and turned in fairly early, eschewing the novelty of having Sky television for the first time in ages.

I awoke at about 0300 with a scream stuck in my throat and the most ghastly noise reverberating through the house. I realised through the fog of sleep that the burglar alarm was going off, and that I had to get to the remote to switch it off quickly. I legged it for the staircase and stumbled down, switching on the sitting-room lights on the way down. No house keys on the dresser, no house keys on the coffee table, I must have left them in the kitchen.

The siren was now blaring right in my ear, making coherent thought extremely difficult. I headed for the kitchen, caught my toe on the top step of three and fell onto the kitchen table. The house keys slid off the table and onto the floor; I pounced on them and hit the kill button on the remote. Blessed silence.

There was no way in this world that I was going to be able to get back to sleep, so I switched on the television. Big mistake.

The first film to which I turned was some totally forgettable drama concerning teenage vampires. Utterly horrified by the blood and violence after one minute of the film (and it was rated '15'), I turned to the next channel. I really was out of luck: the next one down was showing 'The Texas Chainsaw Massacre'.

I ask you, with tears in my eyes, how can people bear to watch such unrequited violence? Or was it just that my nerves were shot, post-burglar alarm? I sat in front of the television, clutching a cold mug of tea, absolutely appalled by the horror on the screen.

I was extremely pleased to see daylight around the shutters, as the thought of a shadowy figure with a chainsaw, waiting on the patio was a little too close to the forefront of my mind.

With a couple of phone calls, I arranged a visit from Frederik Michol, the local electrician, who arrived on the Thursday morning. Fred is a likeable character, the scion of a local family who have looked after the area electrically for the last three generations. He is married to a local psychologist and has two children, a girl of seven and a boy of four.

There was too much snow for Fred to drive his Mercedes to the house, so I met him at the top of the drive and transferred him and his tools into my Jeep. The first sign that things were going wrong was when Fred climbed out of the Jeep, slipped on a patch of ice and landed flat on his back on frozen snow. He lay there for a while, groaned, then eventually came to his feet, stretching his two-meter frame in some pain. I grabbed his toolbox from the back of the Jeep and led him into the house.

The control units for the Wi-Fi alarm system are in the sitting-room, hidden behind a stack of folding patio chairs. I quickly moved the chairs out of the way, a trifle embarrassed by the thick coating of dust on the floor where they had lain for the last year. Fred gingerly lay down on the tiles in order to dismount the control box, instructing me to keep the alarm remote handy to quell any unwanted action by the siren.

Fred was looking fairly comfortable and was starting to undo the mounting screw when I saw a large scorpion ambling towards his left ear. Now, there is a school of thought that dictates that one should not yell a warning as this can increase the fright factor, but that one should give a warning in a calm voice. I am not a believer in this. I shrieked a warning: "ATTENTION, IL Y A UN SCORPION!!!"

62

For a two-meter-tall man, Fred acted with incredible athleticism. He virtually levitated from a prone position on his back to a standing position. The only unfortunate part was that he connected the underside of the stairs with his head on the way up, and left a painful-looking contusion on his forehead.

I dealt with the scorpion quickly and asked whether Fred would like a coffee or anything to settle his nerves. He snarled something at me which I was not particularly keen to have heard, and carried on dismounting the unit. Having discovered that the problem was due to low voltage in a couple of battery packs, Fred was well on the way to solving my problem.

Having replaced the batteries on the two indoor units, it was time to have a look at the outside control, which is fastened to an outside wall just below roof level. I fetched the ladder, and held it firm while Fred climbed up and dismounted the unit. He carefully brought it to earth and took it inside to renew the battery pack. He climbed back up and replaced the screws holding it, at which point the alarm siren went off again.

I can only say that the result was spectacular. Fred seemed to be propelled off the ladder by the loudness of the siren, landing in about half a meter of snow on the patio. I, meanwhile, tried to run inside the house to get to the remote and silence the din, but unfortunately caught my boot on the bottom of the ladder. I went sprawling in the snow, while the ladder slid sideways and eventually fell on top of Fred.

With the repairs now finished, I once again offered Fred a coffee. He shook his head silently and picked up his toolkit, setting off in front of me to the waiting Jeep. We climbed in, and I noticed that Fred was studiously fastening his safety belt although we would travel only 400 meters: he did not trust me. Before we took off, I turned to Fred and asked whether I could pay him in cash. He declined any payment at all, and just indicated that he would like to get back to his car in one piece.

I drove back up the drive as carefully as I could, slipping and sliding a bit on the corners, while Fred hung on for dear life. I deposited him next to his car, thanked him again for his kindness, received a very crooked smile in return, and he was gone, no doubt relieved that he wouldn't be called again for another four years.

February 2012

Cherry Jam
A Tale of Pitiful Incompetence

Summer had come to Provence and, being a landowner, I decided to utilise the benefits of my property.

I have cherry trees, plum trees and apricot trees, virtually none of which has ever been properly picked, and the fruit has often just rotted on the trees. Naturally the birds love me, as do the 'loirs' (thieving, overgrown dormice) that live in my roof and the wasps that can make summer a misery.

The first trees to fruit were the cherry trees, and the branches sagged under the weight of fruit. I am not a great consumer of fruit and the thought of eating fresh cherries more than a couple of times a week was not appealing. So…why not make jam?

It couldn't be that hard. I am a ship's captain with hundreds of thousands of sea miles under my belt; I can operate arcane instruments such as sextants and pelorus, modern stuff like GPS, plotters and radar, surely making jam would be simple?

Oh yeah??

I started by picking all the cherries closest to the ground, about two kilos. I used a knife to pit them, managing to cut myself only once. The job took an age, and was the most ball-achingly boring occupation that I have ever undertaken. I then opened the bible of cookery that resides in my kitchen – Delia Smith's Complete Cookery Course – how could I possibly go wrong?

I brought the cherries to the boil, small amount of water, right amount of confiture sugar, yadda yadda, and then put a small amount on a cooled plate.

It did not set. Merde!

Boiled it again then sort of gave up; put it into jars.

It did not set. Merde again!

A day and a half later the cherries on the tree were carrying on regardless, more and more of them ripening as I watched, so it was time to try again.

This time I equipped myself with a seamanlike array of equipment: a heaving line complete with a curtain weight to throw over branches, a stick with a crook on it for grabbing branches, and a small stepladder to aid my ingress into the tree where I would be able to pick all the cherries so far missed.

The heaving line was most effective, and I managed to throw it over plenty of branches that would have been impossible to access. I picked more and more cherries, filling two plastic bags with the fruit. I sustained one small contusion when the curtain weight bounced off a branch and onto my bald head, giving me a painful but not grievous wound.

I had been loaned a simple cherry pitter, a sort of garlic crusher with attitude, and I used this to great effect. Science is wonderful, but it still took an age to pit the cherries.

The time had come to test the new mix of confiture sugar and lemon juice.

I emptied the jars of previously unsuccessful jam into the large pressure cooker, along with all the new cherries. No water, right quantity of confiture sugar, right quantity of lemon juice, (supposedly endowed with huge amounts of pectin, the element that makes jams set). I brought the pot to the boil, and had started to time it when the phone rang.

I answered the phone, spoke for a shortish time (considering that it was relevant to possible future employment) and then returned to the kitchen.

Oh, merde yet again! Have you ever seen a stove top covered with a sticky mass of sugary cherry compote? It is truly disgusting, and I had to stop all operations until the mess had been cleared up.

Three hours later, in a filthy mood, I once again put the so called 'jam' into the jars.

It did not set.

The next two days were filled with thunderstorms, televisions losing signals at the moment when a winning try was about to be scored, electricity going off when I was in the bath, and various other life-threatening situations.

On the Monday there were again huge clumps of cherries screaming to be picked before the birds got them. I had found a notice in a local sales magazine that advertised a pitting machine for cherries, olives and small plums.

It was a sign.

I hustled down to the village of Puget-Théniers, and lined up with other hopefuls at the truck that was a repository of all sorts of goodies, including the pitting machine. It came in a box, with very complicated instructions on the side. Most impressed, I paid my money and headed for Carrefour, the local supermarket, where I would buy more confiture sugar.

In the supermarket I saw my neighbour, Gilbert, and asked him why my jam had not set.

Big mistake.

Gilbert immediately accosted a large moustachioed lady of senior years, and asked her the question. She rattled off a reply, casting doubts onto the amount of sugar that I had used, but saying that I should boil the jam again, and add more sugar. At this point another lady of equal girth, equal age and superior moustache joined the discussion, and shouted that the first lady's cure was a crock of merde, and that I should add no more sugar, only lemon juice. Things were getting pretty heated, and I caught sight of Gilbert sliding out of the door, miserable coward, leaving me with a veritable riot in the making. I did my best to quieten things, promising both matriarchs that I would try their methods separately and report back. Liar that I am.

I arrived home and got to work. First a T-shirt that was loose around the shoulders and beyond repair, a pair of shorts and sandals. The small stepladder up against the tree, heaving line in my pocket, a plastic bag to hold the cherries, and I was set.

The sun was shining, there was a drone of insects of every size and description, and I was ready for work. I used the stepladder to attain the lower branches of the cherry tree, (funny the way it is not as easy to scamper up a tree at sixty-five years of age!) and found myself a comfortable perch where I could access a lot of the upper branches. I was doing really well, and had about a kilo and a half in the bag when disaster struck.

I felt a twig fall down the wide sleeve of my T-shirt, and scratched at my armpit with my other hand.

It was not a twig, and the wasp stung me with incredible hatred. I screamed like a small girl, lost my balance on the branch and fell out of the tree.

Really pitiful.

There were three lucky breaks in the whole hideous debacle:

Firstly, I only fell a couple of metres.

Secondly, I fell into long thick grass, so injury was unlikely.

Thirdly—and most importantly—there was no one around to laugh at me.

I gathered up my equipment and went into the kitchen to finally bring the whole horrible business to a happy ending. My new cherry pitter was waiting for me, and I set to with a will. The bloody thing only worked on every third cherry, leaving the others with gaping wounds and their stones still extant.

Useless. Twelve euros to the worse.

I boiled up all the previous jam, the new pitted cherries, a load of confiture sugar and the juice of two lemons.

I now have five kilos of very liquid cherry compote. It tastes fantastic, but is the messiest stuff to try and put on toast. Anyone want it?

I think that in future I will give my cherries to one of the village matriarchs, and then happily buy the jam back from them when it is safely 'jarred'.

June 2013

Real Men Make Jam

It was the end of June, Provence was as hot as blazes, and I finally ran out of reasons as to why I shouldn't pick the wild plums from the tree in front of the house and make jam. I had been prevaricating for days, using really pathetic excuses.

"The birds need the food." No, they don't, they are all fat and feathery.

"The plums are not all ripe." Perhaps not, but there are so many ripe ones that they are falling from the tree.

"I should be cutting wood for winter." Rubbish, winter is still five months away.

The real reason for the hesitancy and downright sloth is that I am in complete denial when it comes to admitting that my so called 'jam' always turns out to be more of a very lumpy syrup. It looks great until the jar is rotated and the liquid slops around. It tastes magnificent, but has to be poured onto toast rather than spread; it really has only one use: to be poured over ice cream.

I don't eat ice cream. Rats!

With much foreboding I prepared the kitchen, paper towels by the roll, empty jars all lined up, pressure cooker on the stove, sugar packets prepared (the expensive stuff with extra pectin) etc. Most importantly, the cunningly designed and patented pitter, which is made by Moulinex, and which will one day get me into serious trouble. The problem is that it only removes four pits out of five, and I am just waiting for one of the lucky recipients of my 'jam' to break a tooth on said fifth pit while eating ice cream, and to sue me for some outrageous dental bill.

I have a problem with my shoulders and upper arms that makes working with my arms above my head extremely difficult. I have to lift one arm with the other, grab the end of a branch, use my 95-odd kilos to pull the branch down, swing the unused arm up and pull off as many plums as possible as the arm descends.

If it sounds like hard work, I can assure you that it is. It is also probably most amusing to watch.

I hang a large Carrefour shopping bag around my neck which catches the majority of the plums, the rest are my annual present to the local sounder of wild pigs. They seem to accept it as their due.

So … on this particular morning I surveyed the large number of laden branches, bemoaning the fact that my cousin Robyn's energetic offspring were not available to help. Those two girls, Lara and Geena, would have emptied the tree in a morning and then probably made the jam for me.

I sweated away for an hour, took a bulging shopping bag into the kitchen to begin the industrial side of the business, pitted all the plums, boiled up the pits to get the flesh and juice out of them (and more pectin, if various cookery book authors are to be believed), and then returned to the tree with yet more equipment.

By now I had captured all the easier plums, and needed more height. I took the small step ladder, just three steps, which would allow me access to the higher branches that were covered in plums. I started working away, stripping the plums from the branches, my head in amongst this leafy paradise of fruit, achieving great success.

The thought went through my mind that I was glad that I was not doing this job in the Western Cape at the height of summer, when the chances of finding a 'boomslang' in the tree would be pretty good. I am not good with snakes. I made a mental note to 'Google' the number of fruit pickers from Robertson, Worcester and the surrounding area that were bitten by 'boomslangs' each year.

My head was now covered in bits of twig, and as the twigs are sharp, I had a good few bleeding scratches on my bald pate. These were not painful, but they did attract a number of large flies which irritatingly landed on my head, tickling it, or tried to climb up my nostrils or into my ears. I moved the ladder and started on a really thickly covered couple of branches. The flies came with me.

I was fast running out of patience, trying to swot the flies, getting poked in the eye by twigs, and overheating in the hot stillness of the day.

The ladder, though not high, wobbled dangerously on the uneven ground, and I felt that I probably had enough plums now to fill all the available glass pots. I reached out for one last handful of plums, and as I grabbed them, I saw the snake.

It was small, green, obviously not a 'boomslang', but definitely a snake.

It was all of twenty centimetres from my eyes, which must have been spinning around like tops in my head.

I did what I suspect any red-blooded man would do. I shrieked like a very small girl and fell off the ladder. I landed in a gibbering heap on the ground, my precious plums scattered around me. I checked myself over for injuries and, besides a couple of scratches, I was undamaged. Except for my pride, that is. I put down the shopping bag that was now only half full, righted the ladder, and timorously climbed back up into the tree.

I spotted the snake now about a metre away, it had retreated to a fork in the branch, from where it stared at me and gave a low 'hiss'. As I watched it turned again, and slid sinuously away into the tree.

Enough. I picked up the half-full shopping bag, folded the ladder and wearily headed for the kitchen. When the second load of plums were pitted, I put the pressure cooker onto the stove and fired up the gas; as the fruity mess came to the boil I added exactly the right amount of pectin-rich sugar, brought it all to the boil again, made sure that the sugar was all absorbed, turned off the gas and spooned the jam into the waiting containers.

It didn't set. Big surprise – not!

I did what all great cooks do in moments of disappointment. I looked at my watch and decided that 1200 was the correct time for a dry Martini.

Yes, real men do make jam!

June 2015

71

A Big Day for a Hamster

Brendan Saunders worked as a yacht captain in the late '90s and early in the twenty-first century. He had married a Welsh girl called Rose who had also worked on yachts for many years.

Many couples who had tried to make a home in Antibes found that the yachting industry crept ever-deeper into their private lives while living on the coast, so they decided to move inland: the houses were cheaper, the plots were bigger, and they liked the feel of actually living in France, not some Anglicised suburb where every conversation was about boats.

They had a small daughter called Emily, a sweet child of five years, who was outgoing and adaptable, so there were no worries about her assimilating in a new environment.

Winter weekends were spent touring through the Nice hinterland, known as the Arrière Pays, looking at houses, eating in small and friendly restaurants and making copious notes of their travels.

After a few months, Brendan and Rose had narrowed down their area of interest to the area due north of Nice, along the banks of the Var River. Eventually, with a little help from the owner of the yacht that Brendan skippered, they bought a charming Provençal house on about four acres of land. The house was outside the medieval village of Entrevaux, a stunning little place, complete with a drawbridge over the river and a Vauban fort guarding it from on high.

Emily was enrolled in the local junior school, Rose started teaching English locally, and Brendan drove home from the coast each weekend that he could when he was not on charter. The whole family loved skiing, and the proximity to the ski resorts of the Alpes-Maritimes was an added bonus, one that they utilised to the maximum as winter drew to an end.

Emily loved her new school, and immediately started to make friends with some of the little French girls who lived locally. The

Arrière Pays is a pretty crime free area, and the small girls were able to wander the ancient streets of Entrevaux in safety, visiting each others' houses and playing on the huge expanse of common land between the church and the river.

Rose was an animal lover, and it was a joy for her that she could now have a dog, something that had been impossible when they had been stuck in the apartment in Antibes. She had bought a Springer spaniel that she named Jester, and together they walked for miles through the local forests each morning. Emily also loved animals, and after a year of begging, Brendan brought her back a golden hamster in a cage, from Nice. The hamster was deemed to be French, and was spoken to only in that language. After a period of time, it was decided that the little animal was male, and was accordingly named Jules, which had to be pronounced 'Jool', in the proper French way.

Emily was religious in the care of her charge, cleaning out his cage daily, taking him out in the evening to sit on her lap while she watched a television cartoon before her supper, and feeding him last thing before going to bed. During the day, Jules did hamster-like things: he stuffed his cheeks with anything available, he stayed in shape spinning his wheel and he spent hours in glorious repose.

Jules was a very happy hamster; he was even remembered in Emily's prayers each night.

Life was pretty idyllic, and the family were soon regarded as locals, albeit quite exotic ones, and were accepted in all corners of the village.

The local school taught children only until the age of ten, whereupon they moved on to the middle school just to the south in Puget Théniers. There was a total of 90 children at the Entrevaux school, divided up into five classes, so none of the classes was overly crowded, and the teachers were all local people, young and enthusiastic, who loved the area, the nature and the history.

On the fateful day that changed the lives of the Saunders family forever, it was a fabulous spring day in April. The sun was warm, there was virtually no wind, every bud was budding, blossom on the fruit trees attracted every bee for miles around, and there were young birds everywhere, calling to their parents for food.

The pretty junior schoolteacher, Mademoiselle Lejaune, whose Christian name was Chloe, decided to take the children out onto the grassy common near the church for their morning lessons. She adored everything to do with Mother nature and her incredible workings.

The day before, Chloe had told the children that they needed to bring 'something of interest' to school the next morning, and then talk to the class about it for three minutes, a sort of 'show and tell Française'.

Little Serge had brought some of the dough that his father, the local baker, made into bread each night; Sandrine had dragged an old bed-heater along that had belonged to her grandmother. All the small children produced their 'objects of interest' and gave their explanations as to what they were. Eventually it was Emily's turn, and she rose from her place in the seated ring of children. She shyly reached into her pocket and produced a rather sleepy Jules.

Chloe clapped her hands in delight, and asked if the little creature was tame enough to be allowed to root around in the short grass at the centre of the circle of children. Emily often let him do that in the garden at home, so she put him down and stepped back, preparing herself for her little speech. She had gone onto Google, and had all the facts at her fingertips. The little rodent came from Southern Turkey and Syria, its proper name was Mesocricetus Aurus, and it ate mainly grain and seeds. There were many predators that fed on hamsters.

At that moment, there was a fluting sound from above and a small falcon, one of the natural predators of hamsters, dropped out of the sky. It grasped the unfortunate Jules in its talons and swept back up into the air, giving a lonely cry of triumph as it carried its prize off to feed its young.

Jules was not heard to utter any sound at all, and the children were all silent for a few seconds too.

After the few moments, all hell broke loose. Emily shrieked and clutched at Chloe, who was heard to mumble something about it being natural for a falcon to behave thus. Most of the other children were crying, though one unpleasant child was jumping up and down shouting "Encore, encore!" and waving his arms. Emily turned on him like a tigress and slapped him silly, so he started to cry as well.

It was a day that went down in the annals of Entrevaux as a disturbing time, and some adults even suggested that possibly the children needed 'therapy' to get over the shock. Children bounce back quickly though, and within six months, the wheel in the hamster cage at the Saunder's house was spinning merrily again, being driven by a piebald black and white hamster called Jules Deux.

Jules Deux was, however, never taken to school.

August 2011

An Unusual Wildlife Day in Puget

One of the advantages of living on a secluded estate, with not a single neighbour in sight, is that one's private life is really private.

An early morning joy for me is to be able to 'mark' my territory. I open the French windows out to the patio, which overlooks a wild and unkempt field, take a few deep breaths, and then pee into the long grass a metre below the patio. Strange, you might think, boorish, kinky or lacking in decorum; well, you may be right but I enjoy it, summer and winter.

It is summer now, and the field is full of wildflowers, fruit that has fallen from the wild plum trees, and grass long enough to hide an elephant, albeit a small one. I am waiting for my nearest neighbour, Gilbert, to bring his horses over to board – they look after the long grass.

Yesterday morning I followed my usual ritual, opened the doors, sauntered out still dressed in only a sarong, and started to pee over the side of the patio.

There was something different – a hissing noise which disturbed the normal silence of the morning. I looked down, and the steady stream dried up immediately.

There was a bloody great snake down there, about a metre long, black with yellow markings, and I was pissing on its head.

Now, I know that one should not kill spiders, (it will invariably rain the next day), frogs should be left unharmed, (not sure why, but probably something to do with a shortage of princes), and single magpies should always be addressed as 'Milord' to avoid bad luck. But what, I wondered, was the penalty for peeing on a snake?

On its head.

The snake disappeared into the grass and I'm sure it threw a malevolent glance over its shoulder (shoulder?), as much as to say that it would remember me. I went back in and showered, and all thoughts of the snake were left behind while I planned my day.

My house is old, built of stone, and the roof is a hotchpotch of aging tiles. There is a small rodent known locally as a 'loir' that likes to take up residence in roofs. It is an engaging little animal, a trifle rat-like, but with a full and fluffy tail and huge lustrous eyes. It is nocturnal and hibernates for seven months of the year, for which reason it is known as a 'Siebenschläfer' in German, a 'seven sleeper'.

They are pests.

They use the insulation in the roof to make nests for their loathsome and numerous offspring and they eat the wiring, no doubt purely out of boredom, as they are vegetarian. I have waged war on these vermin for years, using poison which they ignored, trying to block off ingress into the roof, and eventually buying a pellet gun to destroy them as they jumped from the roof onto the electrical cable, which they use as a highway into the woods. The local Frenchmen have started giving me strange looks, which is unsurprising as, whenever they visit at dusk, they find me sitting at the patio table with a bottle of wine and a loaded pistol in front of me. Funny, they seldom visit anymore.

This year there has been a swing to my advantage. A European Wildcat has taken up residence in the woods behind the house, and I have tried to condition him to climb onto the roof at every opportunity. The beginning of the summer showed great success; I occasionally gave the cat a chicken wing on the roof, having put up a plank to make the climb easy for him. There was not a loir to be seen or heard, and the talk in the village was that this year was particularly bad for loirs. I became smug and conceited with my 'oh! so ecological' eradication system. Big mistake.

I think that my rewarding of the cat was a little over enthusiastic, and eventually he started to put on weight. He waited for his chicken wings, which he no doubt found much easier to eat than a loir, none of that fur getting stuck between his teeth. The bloody loirs came back.

So yesterday evening, there I was at dusk, ready with torch and pellet gun, all my senses sharp and expectant. A loir jumped from the roof to the electrical cable, I fired, hit the cable and the loir lost its footing, falling to the ground and scampering across the back yard of the house.

Right past the cat.

The feline imbecile just sat there and watched it run past. I was beside myself with rage, screaming that there would be no more chicken dinners, while the cat slunk off into the darkness.

I retired to the table on the front patio and poured another glass of wine to console myself. I sat there for a while, swatting mosquitoes and listening the mocking laughter of the loirs (or at least that is what it sounded like), when I remembered that I had not closed the sunroof of the car when I came back from the village. Although rain was unlikely, I didn't want any local wildlife taking up residence in the car overnight. I took the torch and walked the thirty metres to the car, which was up in the parking bay, surrounded by the shadows of bushes.

I reached for the car door and one of the shadows moved. It moved at great speed with a shrill squeal, down into the field, kicking up gravel and dust behind it.

I nearly had a baby.

The family of wild boar, locally known as 'sanglier', had been very active for a few days, eating all the fallen fruit and walnuts, but I had not suspected that one was lurking around the car.

Feeling a little jumpy, I headed back down to the patio, only to hear a definite slither of something long and sinuous in the rockery near the kitchen. That was it, enough.

I went inside, locked the door and made a cup of tea to settle down for the evening. I sat down and switched on the television to catch the news. There was the usual unhappy list of atrocities and disasters, which I found too depressing, so I finished my tea and was about to switch off the lights and head for bed, when I saw something move on the surround of the fireplace. How nice. The biggest scorpion that I have seen in ages. I was not in a very merciful mood, so he was dealt with in a violent fashion and chucked into the garbage bin.

I brushed my teeth and headed for bed, while deciding that it was obvious: if you pee on a snake's head, you are in for a fairly interesting wildlife day.

July 2011

Global Warming

I am a European Wildcat, living on the property of a bald-headed idiot outside the village of Puget-Théniers. I am writing this to vent my outrage and frustration at the moronic behaviour of the human race.

Spring came early to Provence this year, and by the last day of February there was blossom on the fruit trees. There were nests of small field mice to be eradicated, the rodent population had increased tenfold, and I was kept busy catching and devouring everything that moved.

Another pleasing aspect of spring is that I can finally shed my winter coat, which I did with the utmost pleasure. Under the long and coarse winter fur, there is a shiny new and stylish coat, which makes me look and act like a different animal. Gone is the hirsute and savage-looking hunter in the snow, Hallo Mr. Smooth! I cannot wait to get down to the village and impress the local moggies with my new sartorial splendour!

And Sandrine! The beautiful Sandrine, with her snowy fur will be enchanted by my tiger-bright and svelte look. Together we will make the sweet music of feline love, and the most awesome kittens, oh yes!

The bald-headed buffoon has been eating plenty of fish lately, and I have been feasting on salmon and trout skin, sometimes the heads as well, so I am in superb condition for this foray into the land of the house-cats, wretched creatures that they are.

I shall time my arrival for the golden hour, that time of day much-beloved by photographers, just before sunset when the soft red tones offer the perfect light for my magnificent colouration to be truly appreciated. Watch out Sandrine!

I washed carefully, then slid out of the forest like a wraith, heading down the hill towards the village. As I trotted down the hill, I noticed my breath started to steam a little; this seemed strange, so I stopped for a second to sniff the air. Rats! It was starting to get colder by the minute. By the time I arrived at the outskirts of the village, clouds had rolled in, and then, Oh the horror! It started to snow.

With sudden clarity I realized what was happening: this was caused by humankind (bald-headed buffoon and his like), and was called 'Global Warming'. For a European Wildcat it spelled disaster.

I was extremely cold without the comfort of my heavy and waterproof winter mantle on my back. I started to shiver, and I felt the cold creeping between my claws. I carried on into the village, determined still to disport myself with the lovely Sandrine, but soon saw that this might not happen. Each window that I passed had a house-cat sitting behind the glass, all looked warm and happy, and many of them gave me smug glances as I stealthily crept past – how I hated and despised them all, and yes, I admit I envied them too.

Eventually I came to Sandrine's house, and there she was in her window, still wearing her pink collar with its little bell. I tried to attract her attention by parading my magnificence up and down the lane, but this is hard to do with the required panache when one is freezing one's goolies off. My whiskers were collecting small icicles, and I was developing a very unimpressive 'drowned-cat' look. I stole a glance out of the corner of my eye, and horror of horrors, Sandrine was laughing at me! At me! – the embodiment of feline grace and beauty! I slunk away, and wearily climbed the hill, heading towards my lair, where I hoped that I could survive this unwelcome cold spell.

On passing the idiot's house, I smelt something wonderful and upon investigation, I found a pile of very small chop bones on the outer windowsill. I settled down and ate them, chewing the morsels of meat off the bones with some enjoyment, despite the miserable cold. When I had finished, I decided to stay on the windowsill for the night, as the idiot had lit a fire, and there was a semblance of heat coming through the window.

A pox on humans and their lousy environmental sense! On the other hand, thank goodness for the buffoon and his fire…

March 2012

Music, Mr. Cat and a Fine Feast

The European wildcat that lives somewhere behind my house has shown a surprising side to his character.

Often I have some music playing when he ventures down to see if there is anything for him to eat on the windowsill of my study, and I have noticed that the type of music seems to affect his mood: If there is a CD of Meatloaf belting out 'Bat out of Hell', or the Rolling Stones performing 'You Can't Always Get What You Want', Mr. Cat is unlikely to even jump up onto the windowsill, so unmoved he seems to be by good rock 'n' roll. If, however, I have something gentler playing such as Mango Groove or Celine Dion, he will show himself and hiss at me to show his desire for something to eat.

The music that seems to really get to him is, surprisingly, classical. I have observed his reaction to various composers, and it is most intriguing.

I suspect that his parentage must have some Germanic genes, as he certainly shows his enjoyment of Bach, Mozart and Schubert by sitting on the windowsill after finishing his meal. The Italian composers do not do much for him: Vivaldi seems to keep him amused for short periods, while Corelli and Puccini send him into a paroxysm of hissing before he quickly departs.

The other night I tried him on Handel's 'Music for Royal Fireworks'. The result was most wondrous. He ate the chicken carcass that I left out for him, settled down on the windowsill and let the music flow over him. It may have been my own enjoyment of the music, or possibly the extra glass of Bordeaux that I had imbibed with my lasagne dinner, but I swear that I saw his tail twitching in time to one of the more expansive horn passages. The moment that the music finished he came to his feet, stretched mightily, gave me a farewell snarl and disappeared into the night.

***

I must mention the lasagne. I bought a large slice from the local butcher, who makes it every three or four days. I had often seen plates of it in his display fridge, and decided that it deserved a trial.

I am a great fish eater, and seldom eat red meat, but this lasagne was superb. I warmed up half of the slice, opened a bottle of good Bordeaux, and settled down to my dinner. It tasted so good that gluttony overcame me, and I warmed up the rest of the slice, poured more wine and thoroughly enjoyed myself.

After dinner, I had some e-mails to send so went upstairs to the study, taking the bottle of wine with me. It was then that I decided to put the Handel CD onto the player and turn up the volume. Mr. Cat duly arrived and I fetched the chicken carcass for him from the kitchen.

I was tired now, and feeling a little 'overdone' in the eating and drinking department (having topped off the lasagne feast with a morsel of strong sheep's cheese to go with the last of the fine Bordeaux). So I quickly bathed and prepared for bed and, making sure that the bedroom window was wide open, fell into my bed, listening with satisfaction to the absolute silence outside. I was asleep within moments, that wonderful deep and dreamless sleep that is so good for us.

I woke up at around one-thirty in the morning, and took a second or two to work out what had disturbed me. Then I heard a noise that alerted me to the fact that the 'sangliers', the local wild pigs, were back and foraging in my garden. I sleepily got out of bed and went to have a look out of the window—not a sanglier to be seen, despite the bright moonlight. I went back to bed, wriggled into a comfortable position, and again heard the strange noises.

It took a few seconds to realise that there were no sangliers or any other wildlife whatsoever, and that the strange animalistic noises were , in fact, coming from my stomach. A surfeit of lasagne and red wine is perhaps not the best regime on which to go to sleep, especially when followed by a capricious sheep's milk cheese.

November 2014

The Urge to Merge

As a genuine European Wildcat, I fear nothing. I am quick, fearsome and incredibly brave. I am also French, so I am not imprisoned by idiotic modesty.

It is late spring, and creatures with real feelings become uncomfortable at this time of year. There is an itch, a sense of discomfort, a gross overload of hormonal activity – basically we need to fuck.

With the onset of this fur-lifting condition I left the safety of the cave in the woods where I live, foregoing the irregular offerings of food from the imbecilic human who lives in the house nearby. He gives me stuff like bones of lamb chops, skin and heads of salmon and trout, and other delicacies from time to time, which make a welcome change to my normal diet of rodents, birds and reptiles.

I headed down the hill towards the village, where there are a host of those poofter creatures that are known as 'domesticated house cats'—pathetic animals that make meowing noises and use their tails to show their state of mind. Amongst them is a particular piece of pussy that I find exceedingly toothsome—she makes my blood race and my genitals throb. Her name is Sandrine, she is a real 'townie', white all over, with long fur. Her owner (hideous, imagine having an owner!) makes her wear a pink collar with a small bell on it.

Oh! but how I long to make that bell rattle as I demonstrate to her the passionate nature of a wildcat!

The usual state of affairs on entering the village was to be hissed at by some of the craven moggies that live there. They are pitiful fighters, full of bombast and spit, I normally stride past them, magnificent in my arrogance, only occasionally do I need to slash a face or shoulder just to make sure that they remember their place. Normally I find that showing them a claw, and threatening to cut off their balls, clears the way for me to continue deeper into the winding streets.

I was led to the area of real down and dirty action by the ridiculous caterwauling of a couple of stiff-legged and posturing so-called tomcats. Clowns. The two of them were trying to impress Sandrine, who was sitting on the steps of the house where she lived. They tried to ignore me for a few moments—I just sat and stared at them. One walked towards me with his fur all bouffant, and his back arched. I waited until he was within range, laid my ears flat and gave him a real growl. As I had expected, he stopped and I leaped forward and gave him both paws, all ten claws extended. He shrieked like a kitten and fell over backwards, one ear lacerated and a clump of his whiskers missing. He and his homosexual buddy raced away, leaving me alone with Sandrine.

It was time to be a lover, not a fighter.

Sandrine watched me with interest, then started to wash behind her ears—this is a typical ruse used by females not wishing to look too 'easy'.

I walked towards her, swinging around at the bottom of the step on which she sat, where I sprayed a generous amount of my strong-smelling essence—some of it actually landed on her tail and paws.

Her reaction was most unexpected. She leaped at me, claws extended with a scream of rage, and slashed me below my right eye.

She then explained, using unladylike language, that her owner had bathed her that very afternoon, and the last thing that she wanted was to be mated and rolled around by a foul-smelling wildcat, who, it seemed, had already pissed her off by spraying her tail and paws.

I was speechless.

This was the most appalling thing to ever happen to me.

It was bad enough that a little housecat should lay a claw on me, but to discover that she had been bathed, and now smelt of some disgusting pharmaceutical product that completely covered her natural scent, well! That was the end.

I wended my disappointed way back up the hill and jumped onto the windowsill of the imbecile's house. It was most gratifying that when he saw me, he noticed my swollen and weeping eye and was immediately concerned. I was given a terrine of some house cat food, rich in liver and vitamins, which hit the spot.

This whole sex business is an extremely over-rated and dangerous activity.

May 2012

The African Curse

I was enjoying a wonderful autumn day in the foothills of the Alpes-Maritimes, about fifty kilometres north of Nice, having recently arrived back from South Africa—a land offering many options for dying before one's time, including suicidal taxi drivers and people who will kill for a cell phone.

The weather was mild; there were patches of blue sky accompanied by brilliant sunshine, though there seemed to be banks of heavier cloud building towards the west.

I am not sure why I am boring myself and my readers with descriptions of the weather, when it has absolutely no bearing on the near-death experience I had that day. Perhaps I am trying to detract from the stupidity and idiocy that I managed to exhibit. Please judge for yourselves.

I have read that more old people die of choking than any other cause. Apparently, choking leads very quickly to the body going into shock, and this leads very soon to death. I am sixty-four years old, certainly not old enough to die of asphyxiation brought on by choking.

Or am I?

I live in a small 'bergerie', a shepherd's cottage, in the hills outside Nice. I have no close neighbours, and have cultivated a local reputation for eccentric and 'curmudgeonly' behaviour. If I were to fall down and break a leg while walking down to my stream, about five hundred metres away, I suspect that I would die of hunger and exposure before being welcomed as a grand 'bonanza' by all the local wildlife, who would surely put my mortal remains to the best possible use. Certainly, there are no concerned people nearby that would either hear my feeble cries, or do anything even if they did hear them.

A fellow who lives at the bottom of the hill, Gilbert, puts two horses out to graze on my land each year, which helps us both. His horses fatten up for winter, and I have a very ecological grass-cutting service which keeps my large field looking respectable. These horses are interestingly named Bambi and Thunder. No, I have absolutely no idea why.

Bambi and Thunder are contained by a temporary electric fence which finishes very close to my patio. They are friendly animals, and have come to regard me as a supplier of carrots and other interesting treats, which I give them on occasion.

The only other regular visitor is a European Wildcat, imaginatively named Mr. Cat. This animal is not a pet, but merely accepts the odd bit of food from what I suspect he thinks of as 'that imbecile in the house'. Me.

On this particular afternoon I settled down to watch a whole swathe of different rugby matches on the television. There were Heineken Cup matches, Curry Cup matches, and even an International between NZ and Australia.

By five o'clock I was fairly hoarse from shouting at the TV screen, and in need of liquids. I poured myself a medium sized Scotch and decided to have a snack with my evening drink.

This was the mistake.

I filled a small ramekin with a particular brand of roasted peanuts that I had bought in South Africa, and popped one into my mouth as I picked up my drink to return to the rugby.

On swallowing, something went wrong, and the peanut ended up in my windpipe. I found that I could not breathe, shout, swallow or shriek. I managed to put the glass of scotch down carefully, clutched my throat and tried to work out what to do.

Now we all know that this is the time for a saviour to inflict the Heimlich manoeuvre on one, even to the point of cracking a rib or two, in order to get the foreign object to be expelled forcibly. Unfortunately, neither of Gilbert's horses has either the brain or the dexterity to have learned anything so vital. The Wildcat, who was sitting in the sun on the upper patio, has neither the physique nor any interest in medical matters, besides which, a dead 'imbecile' of my size would make him a very happy cat over the winter months. So, no Heimlich manoeuvre, what next?

By now I was beginning to panic, just a little, and I tried to think of ways to very quickly rid myself of the peanut, realising that if I did not, I would soon pass out and then expire. Thoughts flitted through my mind: I have been shot at, I have been knifed, and I have survived savage gales and mountainous seas. Please God, let me not meet death through something as ignominious and puerile as a roasted South African peanut!

I rushed outside and started to throw myself repeatedly onto my back on the grass. The first effort was fairly good, and I thought that I felt the nut move slightly, but this could have been imagined, as the piece of grass that I had thrown myself onto had a large rock hidden from view. I caught the large rock in the middle of my back, eliciting an attempted scream of agony, and I think it was this that shifted the peanut a minuscule amount. My next effort was better, and I felt the nut move once more. The third attempt was spectacular, even though my vision by then was fading, and everything was seen in shades of grey. As my back struck the ground the peanut shot out of my mouth, and I lay there heaving and panting like a landed fish.

I heard a whickering over to my left, and saw that Bambi was watching me over the electric fence. There was no concern or worry in the horse's expression, just a wordless question, "Where are the carrots?"

Mr. Cat was now sitting up near the woodshed, and his expression said something totally different: "Rats! Now I have to worry about food for the winter."

I staggered into the house, shutting the wildlife outside, settled down with my scotch and the TV, and decided that 'Africa Wins Again' is a very true saying. The Dark Continent always has devious ways of dispatching people with extreme prejudice ...

October 2013

The Saga of the Toe

On a beautiful March afternoon during a trip to South Africa, I was briskly heading out onto the balcony in order to enjoy the view of False Bay while I did some letter writing. As befitted the glorious day I was in T-shirt and shorts. I was also barefoot.

I strode out of the French windows, or at least that was the idea. The window was closed. All ninety-five kilos of momentum was absorbed by my big toe making solid contact with the glass, which seemed to bow outwards but did not break.

I howled.

I fell to the floor and held my throbbing extremity with both hands as the howls turned to snivelling and foul language. Within ten minutes the pain had all but disappeared, and I carried on with my day in only very mild discomfort.

I went to bed that night at a reasonable hour, and slept through until about 0630, when I realised that something was wrong. I moved my legs and let out an expletive, which poor Sune did not appreciate at that time in the morning. I pushed the sheet off my legs and stared in consternation at the large, pale boxing glove that seemed to have been joined to my ankle during the night.

My foot was so swollen that the four lesser toes looked a bit like a nanny goat's udders in dire need of milking. I staggered out of bed and made my way to the shower, quickly realising that I could put no weight whatsoever on the sole of my foot, so I had to walk on the outside edge. This made me look either drunk, imbecilic or at the very least someone to avoid. It probably did not help that I was muttering under my breath, again using foul language. (I did not notice this on the way to the shower, but later at the Somerset Mall, where I staggered past Woolworths looking like an inebriated and foul tempered octogenarian crab. Mothers drew their revolting offspring out of my way, and even evil-looking young men with shaven heads avoided making eye contact with me.)

The next day I went to Medi-Clinic, where X-rays were taken and I saw a young lady doctor. She was full of sympathy, and taped the toe to its neighbour, but told me that there was nothing else to be done.

A week passed, while I became even more curmudgeonly and foul-tempered than usual. I found that driving was extremely painful, and that I seemed to take it out on other drivers, pedestrians and especially cyclists. I eventually went to see my GP, Dr. Rosslee. The doctor is a very attractive lady who managed to show some sympathy between giggles. She was of the opinion that the toe would take weeks to heal, and that it was, besides having received trauma, arthritic.

Well, as you can imagine, this was just too much—after all, at only sixty-four, I am much too young to have an arthritic toe. She gave me an injection in my backside, and told me to be patient. Over the next three weeks the traumatised toe responded to treatment and seemed to be on the mend.

I always used to sneer at news reports that some rugby star was out of the team for five weeks because of an injury to a toe. I sneer no more.

My return flight to France was most interesting. I had a decent aisle seat, a suitably silent and normal-sized gentleman sitting next to me, and I was looking forward to a restful night and an uneventful trip. On arrival in Dubai however, I realised that all was not well, and that I was going to have trouble getting my shoe back on. Eventually, after much pushing and moaning, the shoe was on, and I was able to hobble along through the terminal to the lounge, where I took three large Scotches for medicinal reasons. The lay-over was seven hours—far too long—but I was pretty comfortable what with the Scotch, the Voltarin and a couple of heavy-duty painkillers.

The flight from Dubai to Nice takes six hours, and I did not dare remove my shoe, so I arrived in a fair amount of agony. My temper was not improved by the late arrival of the luggage to the carousel—how is it that Nice takes longer to unload luggage than anywhere in Africa? (On reflection, I suppose that it is possible that in Africa they are keen to get it off the plane in order to see if there is anything worth stealing.)

Because of the slow luggage I missed the bus that would have taken me directly to Puget-Théniers, and had to take a taxi to the train station. The driver seemed surprised when I did not tip him, and even more surprised when I harangued him at some length on the outrageous price for the short distance. He gave a Gallic shrug, dropped my bag in the gutter and spat on the sidewalk. My blood boiled.

I had another hour to wait for the train, and found a bench to sit on, from which I sent out extra-sensory thoughts to keep the small children and their football away from my foot. The thoughts were not powerful enough, and a disgusting little fellow tripped over my foot while I dozed.

I shrieked.

I remonstrated with the mother, and explained that her parasitic little bundle of joy had stamped on my broken toe. She was totally without sympathy, and gave me a look normally reserved for paedophiles and lepers, while her loathsome offspring sniggered from behind her huge derrière.

Three days later I was still struggling to walk and, as well as I know my house, I still constantly found new places to catch the toe: on a stair, the corner of a mat, the leg of a table.

I eventually phoned Dr. Rosslee in Cape Town, a much cheaper option than seeing one of the local sawbones, most of whom I would not trust to tend to a dead body. The good doctor basically told me to man-up, grow a pair and keep taking the Voltarin.

It is now ten weeks since the unfortunate accident, and I still get twinges in the toe from time to time. I have a ghastly feeling that it is more painful on the morning after a convivial evening spent imbibing red wine with friends.

Gout? No more red wine and other delights? Surely not, I think I would prefer the arthritis!

April 2013

Fluff

Picture this: a warm and balmy evening some 5000 years ago; Ug, after a successful hunt, goes to the river to wash off some mammoth blood. He removes his antelope skin clothing and enters the chilly waters, where he blows and splashes while revelling in the thought of the feast that the community will have that night. Who knows? Perhaps Mrs. Ug will put out in honour of his hunting brilliance.

He leaves the water and settles down on the bank, rolling around in the warm grass to dry his body. This is always a good time to examine the body for lice, ticks, or any other freeloading passengers. He wrinkles his brow in puzzlement, as he pulls from his belly button a small wad of fluff.

The fluff is blue in colour.

Now, the antelope skin that Ug wears is not blue. Mrs. Ug has no blue coloured fleeces or skins in the cave, and in fact the only blue coloured fur that Ug has ever seen was from a small animal (now known as a blue duiker) which a very nubile lady across the valley uses to make very soft karosses, which she sells for huge numbers of clams or large amounts of mammoth meat.

Ug is very inquisitive. He carefully wraps the bit of blue fluff in a leaf, dresses himself in his antelope skin and heads for home. On arrival, he first tells Mrs. Ug all about the hunt, while he gets his finger paints ready and starts to add to the story of his life on the wall of the cave. Mrs. Ug is delighted with the idea of a feast that night, and runs to the next-door cave to discuss with Mrs. Ook what they are going to wear.

Ug finishes the chapter of the mammoth hunt on the cave wall, and is cleaning his fingers, when Mrs. Ug returns. She idly picks through his impedimenta, and sees the carefully folded leaf, opens it and pulls out the wad of blue fluff. She asks, in a mystified voice, what this is.

Ug, wiping his hand clean on a stone, explains that he found it in his belly button.

There is a moment of heavily charged silence, sparks seem to fly out of Mrs. Ug's eyes, and in a cold and savage voice she asks if the mammoth hunt had taken place on the other side of the valley. Oblivious to her insinuation, Ug admits that yes, that is indeed where they had cornered and then taken down the mammoth, and that was where two of his fellow Neanderthals had met their end.

Mrs. Ug went for him like a tigress.

So, after the hunt he had disported himself with the hussy who made the blue coloured karosses had he? He thought that such a great hunter should be allowed to transgress like this did he? Well, let him understand properly, that the curtain of her sleeping shelf was closed to him for ever. He could go back across the valley and roll around in blue fur if he wanted, but this side of the valley would afford him no warmth, comfort or recreation!

Ug was speechless (even more so than the average Neanderthal), and tried vainly to explain that Mrs. Ug had the whole thing wrong.

I would like to think that eventually all was peaceably sorted out, but I doubt it.

Now this whole tale came to me while I was sorting out the laundry on the boat that I am baby-sitting in Barcelona. I had just taken a load of sheets and pillowcases out of the tumble drier, decided that they could do with another cycle, and replaced them. The tumble drier refused to start, and a little 'beep,' accompanied by a read-out on the display, alerted me to the fact that the filter needed cleaning. Now the filter had been scrupulously cleaned the day before, and only white cotton sheets had been washed since.

So how come the fluff in the filter was all blue?

Invariably, when fluff is taken from a washing machine, a tumble drier, the underside of a dog's blanket, the fluff is always blue.

I feel that this question deserves some real respect, along the lines of: Why are we here? Or, Are we the only inhabited planet?

'Why is fluff always blue?' deserves a place in there with the great mysteries of life and the universe.

(And I suspect that it was at least 1000 years before a future Mr. Ug found the courage to ask his good lady the colour of the fluff in her belly button!)

The Rodents' Revenge

I consider myself to be something of a conservationist in most situations. I don't allow hunting on my land, and I enjoy having the animals around—though I am partial to enjoying a meal of 'Daube de Sanglier' (wild-boar stew) or 'Filet de Cerf' (venison) in one of the local hostelries from time to time.

The local foxes have learned that they will usually find a chicken bone or the head of a trout outside my house late in the evening, and for a couple of years I supported the lifestyle of a genuine European wildcat, despite being hissed and spat at each time that he accepted an offering of food on the windowsill.

The only animal that I do my best to eradicate is the lowly 'loir'. This little rodent is a sort of overgrown dormouse, with large and lustrous eyes, a soft grey pelt with a white front, and a long furry tail. Extremely attractive little animal though it is, it is a veritable terrorist in the home and in the areas around the house. My house has a large walnut tree right outside the back door, and a healthy fig tree at the side. The walnut tree produces very well, and the walnuts supplied are extremely tasty.

I have eaten four of them in the twelve years that I have owned the house.

I cannot blame this entirely on the loirs, as the red squirrels also raid the tree every year, but they seem to do it with some sense of moderation, and as the total squirrel population is only about ten, I can well afford to let them harvest and hide what they need for the winter. The loirs, however, will bite into each walnut, knock them off the branches, and then discard them, wasting dozens each night. As the loir population is legion, the huge number of nuts destroyed can only be imagined. The loirs also eat the figs, usually taking a single bite out of four or five before nearly finishing one.

It makes my blood boil.

The loirs have decided that the space between the ceilings of my upper rooms and the tiles of the roof is the best location for them to reside. Here they are protected from cats, owls, and just about all predators (although I remember one wonderful year when a large and hungry 'couleuvre'—a local, non-venomous snake—attained the roof-space by way of the fig tree, and caused terror and consternation among the loirs. Very satisfying.) The most aggravating of all the loirs' habits, is that they will nibble the electrical cables in my ceiling space. I have a feeling that they do this out of boredom or perhaps a diet of walnuts and figs needs plastic sheathing as a supplement?

When the wildcat was around he made a good job of keeping the numbers down, and I would smile beatifically when, late at night, I heard shrieks of terror from the loirs as the cat ran across the roof to scrag a victim with his murderous claws. But the cat has gone, either prey to a larger predator, or else to a place where he doesn't have to cough up furballs constantly from a diet of small, furry beasts.

The loirs are nocturnal, and I have discovered that they exit the roof space a little while after dusk, disport themselves on the tiles for a while, and then set off foraging, using the trees and the overhead electrical flex as a highway. I have, over the last few years, perfected a method of immolating them as they leave the protection of the house. I suddenly switch on the outside flood light by remote, and pick them off with an air-rifle while they are transfixed and unable to move. About thirty or forty have met their end this year in the above manner, and (in line with my eco principles) they have been laid out for the foxes, and accepted gratefully. I did suggest to my neighbor after a bottle or two of 'rouge', that I should start skinning them and using the pelts to make a waistcoat, but Gilbert did not think that this was a tasteful idea.

The loirs have got smart, and the message seems to have got around, that it is dangerous to 'freeze' when the light is switched on, so I came up with a new and cunning scheme to carry on the extermination. Loirs apparently love apples, and the local apple farmers have a torrid time when they put the apples in the barn for the winter. I first cut some rounds of apple, and nailed them to the walnut tree in full view from my bedroom window. For three nights I did this, and each morning the apple had been devoured. The stage was set.

I adjusted the furniture in my bedroom so that I had a comfortable seat on the teak chest in front of the window. I nailed two more pieces of apple to the walnut tree before dusk and took the air rifle, lead pellets and a powerful torch upstairs. I left a small piece of paper, the size of a loir's head, next to the apple on the tree, and sighted in the air rifle. I donned a dark-coloured sweatshirt, a pareo (for comfort), and furry boots to keep my extremities warm. The light on the corner of the house lit up the tree, making the apple rings glow slightly. The light was not good enough for shooting, hence the powerful torch ready to hand. I imbibed no wine or coffee with my dinner, to prevent any notion of the 'shakes', and took up my position silently just after dusk.

I sat there with the patience of a praying mantis, ears and eyes alert for a scuffle or a fast-moving shadow. After about forty minutes there was a scrabbling sound and a muted squeak from the roof above me. I went through my practiced manoeuvres, pulling the rifle in to my shoulder with my right hand, the barrel resting and steady on the windowsill, while with my left hand I reached for the torch and held it so that the beam would light up both the apple rings and the rifle sights. There was a furtive shadow of movement at the fork of the tree below the apple; I switched on the torch and swung it sideways to attain the correct position.

I then dropped the bloody thing out of the window.

As it fell, I made a despairing grab for it, the rifle automatically swung away to the right, and my clutching fist pulled the trigger.

There was the whine as the slug ricocheted off the side of my Jeep, and the torch clattered onto the porch roof, before crashing down onto the patio table. From above me on the roof I distinctly heard what I can only presume was rodent hilarity. The loirs had the last laugh.

Sept 2017

Lufthansa

I usually fly from Nice to Munich around the 27th December each year in order to spend New Year with my father's old widow, Lisl. It is a quick and easy trip: I drive down to Nice airport from my house in the hills, leave the car in a long-term car park and board a direct flight to Munich. The flight is a mere two hours, and almost always runs with true Teutonic efficiency. The stewardesses are slightly older and inclined to be a trifle serious – one is certainly not going to ask for anything that is not offered from the trolley. On arrival at the J.S. Strauss Airport in Munich, I am always impressed by the cleanliness, the friendliness and the overwhelming efficiency of the place. To give you some idea of the differences between my point of departure and point of arrival, it is almost necessary to sprint between the aircraft and the baggage hall to arrive there before your bag is put to one side as being 'unclaimed' (*nicht abgeholt*). On arrival in Nice however, one has time for a leisurely stroll down the Promenade des Anglais followed by a coffee and a croissant before your bag snails its way out onto the baggage carousel.

(I apologize for my digression, but I have always wanted to have a go at the French baggage handlers…)

The route from the arrivals hall to the car hire desks is clearly marked, and there are moving walkways that whisk you along at autobahn speeds. People stand on the right-hand side of the walkways, so that those in a hurry can walk past with ease – *alles in ordenung*! The car hire desks are all gathered in a single clump, and the young people working there all seem to speak at least four languages. (Hmm, don't get me started on the intractability of the French people who do the same job in Nice – they are usually too busy talking to each other to take any interest in helping a poor tired traveller to find his booking.)

Driving in Germany is always exciting. One stutters along the wide, well-maintained and beautifully sign-posted autobahns at a daring 130 kph, while Mercedes, Porsches and BMWs flash past in the fast lane doing in excess of 200kph. Eventually one grows a pair, and the speedometer climbs to a dizzy 170kph, but the German Road Warriors still howl past, seemingly sucking the paint off your car in the vortex that they cause.

A very pleasant drive of an hour and a half, (or 190kms in German) and I arrive in Berchtesgaden, the most Bavarian of all Bavarian towns. Lisl has lived there since 1962, first with my father, and then staying on after his death in 1993. Lisl is a very well-born Austrian lady, but she loves being amongst the mountains and the valleys where she and my father were so happy. The town is quaint to the point of 'kitsch' - there are numerous gentlemen of all ages wandering around in leather trousers, long socks and green felt hats with wild-pig bristles in the hatbands. The waitresses in the frequent 'gasthausen' and 'wein stubern' all wear the 'dirndl', a very attractive national costume designed to push a girl's bust out like a pouter pigeon, and give her a wasp-like waist which seems likely to result in serious internal injury.

I normally stay with Lisl for four or five days, taking her out to lunch at her favourite local 'gasthausen', and eating our evening meal together at home around six o'clock. A lady of ninety-four years needs her sleep. Lisl drinks a quarter-litre of white wine with her lunch every day, and another half-litre with her evening meal at home. At ninety-four, her mental capacity is quite astonishing, as are her eyesight and her hearing. It is only unfortunate breaks to her femur that leave her a bit incapacitated. Obviously, a bottle of wine per day is good for one.

My return journey to my home is normally as uneventful as the outbound journey. This year I dropped the car off at Munich airport around ten in the morning, then made my way to the departure gate, where I was pleased to see a fairly small group waiting to board - more chance of an empty seat next to me. I had an aisle seat as I usually prefer, and made my way to my place, 22C, sat down and immediately closed my eyes.

The next ten minutes passed quite quickly, people found their seats, realised their mistakes and had to move, couples argued about who would sit next to the window, and joy of joys, no-one took the window seat next to me. There was a bit of a hiatus when everyone was seated, and I wondered why the doors had not yet closed.

Eventually there was the sound of voices, and I opened my eyes to behold a trio hurrying down the aisle. In the lead was a fat child of about four years old, with a piercingly loud wheedling voice. Behind him was his Valkyrie mother, a tall and blonde Germanic woman, her statuesque and well-upholstered form barely contained in black tights with thigh-high boots, and her Rubenesque upper body wrapped in a waist-length fur of some benighted small animal. She was followed by a mild looking gentleman whom I did not place as the revolting offspring's father: he said not a word at any time, and seemingly had no interest in the later behaviour of said disgusting child.

The family found their seats some way behind me, and I went back to studying the inside of my eyelids, happy in the knowledge that I did not have to pretend to be polite to a neighbouring passenger.

Truly it is satisfying to be a curmudgeon.

There was the drone of the pilot's voice, followed by the sleep-inducing rush of acceleration and then the feeling of the first gentle banking of the aircraft as it turned out over the Alps to the south. I was left undisturbed, and snoozed quietly while others were given their poisonous sandwiches and choice of beverage.

I was rudely awakened by an ear-splitting shriek somewhere towards the front of the aircraft. The aforementioned loathsome fat child had apparently evaded the clutches of his incapable mother and set off on a tour of destruction. The boy seemed to delight in running up the aisle and then letting out a banshee-like yell right in the ear of some poor and unsuspecting passenger, such as the elderly lady a few rows in front of me. His mother got out of her seat and went up the aisle to collect him, cooing all sorts of calming words, and calling him her 'Liebe Bruno'.

Well, Bruno was not having any of it. As he sprinted up towards the stewardess station, his mother had to extend her meaty legs to catch up with him. She dragged him back to his seat while he shrieked and yelled. We other passengers looked at each other with much rolling of eyeballs and shaking of heads. Bruno was eventually quietened, I suspect by liberal application to his fat little lips of large quantities of 'Sacher Torte', 'Schokoladenkuchen' or other delights. I drifted off back to sleep.

Sometime later I was awakened again. This time the shriek came from right next to my ear, and I can only blame my instantaneous reaction to pure shock and fright. My eyes shot open and I took in the vision of this nasty child grinning at my discomfort, my immediate response was to give him the works: teeth, mad eyes, bristling beard and an animal howl that actually scared me too.

The results were nothing short of spectacular.

Bruno tried to leap backwards from this unexpected assault, caught his heel and banged his head into the ergonomically designed armrest on the seat opposite. He then fell to the floor in a quivering and shaking heap, while making a sort of keening cry.

The Valkyrie was by his side in a trice, and she looked at me as though I had grievously assaulted her parasitic little bundle. I decided that this was a good time to forget all my bad German and rely on fast intervention by the cabin crew. My neighbour on the opposite side of the aisle mumbled that the kid had got his just desserts, and the blonde immediately turned upon him like a rattlesnake. Luckily, one of the stewardesses came hurrying down the aisle, and asked the mother and child to go back to their seats, as the seat belt lights had come on. I could hear the Valkyrie rattling on to the stewardess behind me: was there nothing to be done to prevent people from scaring her delicate child; look, her poor child had wet his pants; she was going to put in a formal complaint to the airline; was the stewardess not going to censure the ugly old man who behaved so badly? I sat back in my seat, exchanged lofty and knowing smiles with a number of passengers in my immediate vicinity, and again closed my eyes.

On landing, I made my exit quickly, mumbling an 'auf wiedersehen' to the two flight attendants who were busy briefing the captain on what had transpired. The captain gave me an inscrutable look as I passed, and—as I have not yet been banned from ever flying with Lufthansa again—I suspect that he was sympathetic to my case.

Call it sheer funk, but I decided to use the men's room in the baggage hall for a longish time, while I waited for the Valkyrie and her spawn to get their luggage and disappear. By the time I crept around the corner, I just caught a flash of the family exiting the baggage area – I was safe. I left the airport, picked up my car and drove home, satisfied that the honour of adults everywhere had been upheld.

January 2014

The Dangers of a Rural Life

The end of summer is approaching in Puget-Théniers, and I am trying to get all sorts of things crossed off the worklist before I leave for South Africa.

My neighbour, Gilbert, has put up the electric enclosure and introduced his two horses and a donkey into my field. This works well on all fronts: the beasts get to eat a whole load of good grass before the onset of autumn, my field gets 'mown' and fertilised and, as recompense for the water that the beasts drink, Gilbert sweeps my chimney before winter—a very satisfying and mutually useful arrangement.

The younger horse, Thunder, has a penchant for escaping whenever he can, to the point where he would finally ignore the electric fence entirely. The fence used to be powered by a 12-volt battery which was charged by a solar panel. The jolt that it gave the horses (and me on a few occasions) was pretty severe, but Thunder reckoned the few moments of freedom when he could bury his greedy muzzle in my herb garden made it worthwhile.

This year Gilbert has upped his game, and the electric fence is now powered from the mains plug in the garden shed, turning it into a serious piece of constraining equipment. On the odd occasion that I have observed the donkey carelessly touching the electric tape, he has jumped incredibly high, shrieked loudly, and taken off across the field.

Very satisfying.

This morning I decided to try and sort out a problem with my septic tank, which has been making my bath gurgle each time one of the toilets is flushed. The problem is fairly obvious—the breather pipe from the tank has become disengaged, probably due to the attentions of one of the deer which frequent the property. They like to scratch themselves on all sorts of upright objects: trees, walls, and breather pipes for septic tanks. Unfortunately, I have been unable to find the aperture into which the pipe is to be relocated, and I suspect that it has filled in, stopping any ingress of air. I have wasted hours in conversation with the builder who installed the tank, but he has no recollection of the position of the breather, as it was installed over twelve years ago.

I armed myself with a machete and a solid steel-tipped staff, and planned my expedition. First, I filled the horses' water drum, then I switched off the plug in the shed to incapacitate the electric fence. I abandoned my usual open sandals and donned a pair of sensible boots as protection against the brambles, and set off down the hill to the area of the septic tank about a hundred metres distant.

The horses and the donkey (especially the donkey) watched with great interest as I swung my leg over the electric tape of the fence. I swear I saw the disappointment in the donkey's face when I didn't scream or thrash around.

I arrived at the first of the manhole covers, which was still fairly visible, and I started to clean around it, ripping out weeds and shrubs, and scraping away the accumulated earth. I was conscious of a tickling on the back of my left leg, which quickly turned to a sharp stinging sensation.

Fire ants.

These loathsome little insects really bite hard, and I had disturbed their nest, so they were particularly vicious. I believe the watching donkey had a moment of pure joy when he saw me leaping around like a dervish while swatting my legs. I eventually divested myself of the attacking horde, and moved on to search for the second manhole cover, as the breather socket should be close to this.

Twelve years of grass (well fertilised) and brambles cover the whole area, so it is decidedly hard to find a piece of concrete only a metre across. I hacked and dug, but to no avail, and after about forty minutes of fruitless manual labour, I was covered in sweat and my sense of humour was long gone.

A great patch of thick brambles and saplings were close by, and I wondered whether the tank could have been situated there twelve years ago, when there would have been very little vegetation. I swung a leg over the electric tape to reach it, and an express train hit my most delicate genitals, accompanied (I am sure) by a faint smell of burning.

I screamed very loudly. I fell on the ground and rolled around with both hands clutching my groin. This was highly dangerous, as my machete was still attached to my wrist by a thong. I lay there moaning and snivelling for a few seconds, when I realized that my neck and arms were stinging—yes, another nest of fire ants.

The two horses and the donkey chose this moment to wander over and look at me. If there is any such thing as equine laughter, I am sure that it was then that I heard it. I slowly got to my feet, savagely promising a trip to the glue-factory for all three animals, and tried to get my act together. I picked up my dropped staff, brushed off the rest of the ants, and made my way up the hill towards the house. I had to negotiate the fence at the top and so, in a blue funk, I lay on my belly and started to crawl under it like a snake. One of the horses had followed me up, and at this very moment he chose to put a damp and velvety nose on the back of my knee.

I shrieked again … and then yet again as I rose onto my knees and caught the electric tape across my back. Eventually I was clear, and I tottered towards the shed to try and determine what had transpired.

There stood Gilbert. He was quite irate that I had switched off the fence (… his horses could have escaped, he relied on me to keep everything secure etc. etc...)

He suddenly became aware of the murderous look in my eye, and registered the fact that I was clutching a machete in my shaking hand. His diatribe died away to silence. I recounted to him what had happened when he had re-connected the electricity to the fence. He put his head back and roared with laughter … Gilbert is truly a man devoid of compassion.

Worse was to follow: his bloody donkey heard the row, and joined in with a series of 'hee-haws' that sent Gilbert into a further paroxysm of mirth.

Being well into a bottle of rosé wine as I write this, even I have now started to see the humour.

I still want to send the bloody donkey to the glue-factory.

September 2016

Lockdown in France

I have now been home in France for seven days. The lockdown to control the Covid-19 coronavirus does not really affect me, as I am inclined to stay fairly solitary whenever I am back here. I revel in the silence and privacy of my property, and am very content with my own cooking, my own choice of music and TV programmes and, most of all, my own company.

I find that I do talk to myself a bit, but usually it is a burst of self-directed foul language that erupts whenever I do something intensely stupid – which happens most days, in fact.

Here in France, the lockdown is fairly dictatorial. One needs a permit to go to the supermarket or pharmacy, the only two shops allowed to open. There are police in evidence around the village, and roadblocks on the national road from Nice but, in my neck of the woods, there is no one. I am in the fortunate position of being able to walk for a couple of kilometres without leaving my land, and without seeing or hearing another soul.

One of the first effects of the lockdown that I've noticed, is the lack of contrails in the sky. The sky is clear and blue in good weather and, with so few flights now, there is no sound of aircraft climbing out of Nice. I used to hear them when the wind was from the south, as Nice is only 50 kilometres away.

One of the unfortunate effects of being in lockdown, is that my niggling sciatica cannot be attended to, as my excellent local chiropractor is not allowed to open his 'cabinet' (as alternative practitioners' rooms are known in France). As a result, I walk like an octogenarian crab, and can become quite grumpy. I decided to try some 'self-treatment'.

To this end, I dragged out my 'back swing' machine, otherwise known as an inversion table. This remarkable piece of equipment is designed to gently stretch the spine and hips. It is adjustable, so one can set it up to perfectly suit one's height and weight.

Having strapped the feet into padded restraint, you lean back against the inclined table. Slowly raising the arms changes the weight distribution, and the stretcher gently swings over backwards, allowing the body to hang, suspended by the ankles. The body weight helps to straighten and stretch the spine and torso.

In another life, when I was fairly fit and 'fris' (strong), I used to do sit-ups from this suspended position. At this present time in life, I suspect that would result in a hernia or worse.

I set up the infernal machine in my study area, locked my ankles to the padded bars, leaned back against the stretcher, and slowly raised my arms. At this point things started to go wrong.

I suspect that the shape and weight distribution of my body has changed radically since I last used the machine. Of course, it only occurred to me that I probably should have changed the settings **after** I had started to get into trouble.

My arms were only halfway raised when gravity took over with some force, and the stretcher suddenly flipped over at great speed, leaving me hanging upside down. This was fine, and I did some gentle stretching, and some twists from side to side. I hung there quite comfortably for a while, until I started to feel some real pressure behind my eyeballs, and a sort of ringing in my ears. I reached for my thighs with both arms, expecting to feel the stretcher starting to return to its rest position, as the weight distribution changed.

Nothing happened.

I tried to lift myself up by putting my hands on the floor and pushing. There was some movement of the stretcher, but no swinging back into where I wanted to be. I knew very well that I could scream and yell for as long as I wanted, but no bastard was going to hear me.

I realized that my kikoi (which I wear in bed) had fallen off. It was lying on the floor, and I wondered whether I could put it around my waist while upside down. The thought struck me that Anita, my long-suffering housekeeper, would not be coming for her usual weekly visit until the coronavirus had finished. She would visit in one month? Three months? Who knows? I could imagine the poor lady's distress on finding a naked cadaver hanging upside down, his eyeballs on the floor beneath him, and in a nasty state of decomposition.

With a certain amount of panic, I tried to claw my way towards the top edge of the stretcher, to no avail. I next tried to push the bottom of the supporting frame, thereby allowing the stretcher to move in the right direction. A little success and, with some extra effort and plenty of the aforementioned foul language, grunting and heaving, I eventually got the stretcher to a horizontal position. From there it was easy, and I found myself standing on the footrests, blinking away tears and catching my breath.

I have since changed the height setting on the footrest, and when I tried the machine again (very carefully), it worked like a dream.

I still have sciatica.

March 2020

PART TWO

AFRICAN ADVENTURES

Arnhem to Windhoek

The date was the 24th September 1944. The small Dutch town of Arnhem was being blown apart by German efforts to dislodge a stubborn band of British airborne troops.

One of the units represented in the beleaguered town was the Glider Pilot Regiment, and Lieutenant Gillian Maclaine of Lochbuie, commander of "F" Squadron, No. 2 Wing of that regiment, was heartily tired of the lack of food, the constant bombardment, the lack of sleep and most of all the absence of any tobacco.

The airborne force of paratroopers and glider-borne troops had been holed up in Arnhem since the 17th September. They had brought with them stores to last only three days, as they expected to find fairly weak German opposition, and anticipated being joined by American, Canadian and British relieving forces very quickly. Unfortunately, they ran into a large SS Panzer division, which, combined with the bad weather that kept the relieving troops in England, really messed up the plans.

Lieutenant Maclaine was summoned by the officer commanding the defence of the Arnhem bridge, and he scurried over to the building that had been taken over as the local HQ. The CO, Brigade Major Hibbert, asked Maclaine to walk out and meet a German officer who had come halfway across the bridge under a white flag of truce.

When they met in the middle of the bridge, the German officer explained in excellent English that he had come to discuss the surrender. Lieutenant Maclaine replied that the British did not have enough troops to accept the German surrender, as they would never be able to guard them all!

The German smiled in appreciation of the British humour, said that he was sorry that there was going to be more death and bloodshed, gave the young British officer two packets of cigarettes, and walked back to restart the bombardment.

Lieutenant Maclaine made his way back to the British HQ, reported to Major Hibbert, and returned to his unit further along the northern riverbank where he shared out the cigarettes with his men.

Glider Pilot Regiment suffered enormous losses, with 219 killed and another 532 either captured or missing. A further 511 were able to get across the Rhine either by swimming, or by being picked up in canvas assault boats. Maclaine was eventually one of the few Glider Pilot Regiment men to be successfully withdrawn from Arnhem.

Maclaine emigrated to South Africa after the war with his wife and only son. He ran a company based in Durban which distributed all of Seagram's liquor in Southern Africa. This position necessitated a fair amount of travelling around the area, and he was a regular visitor to South West Africa (now Namibia), Rhodesia (now Zimbabwe), Mozambique and Angola.

In 1968 Maclaine was in Windhoek, the capital of South West Africa, and was enjoying a drink in the bar of the Holiday Inn before dinner. He glanced across the room and saw a familiar face at a table in the corner. He called the barman, and asked for a packet of twenty cigarettes and a Scotch to be served to the gentleman sitting at the corner table. The waiter dutifully carried the tray over to the table indicated, and explained that a man at the bar had sent over the cigarettes and the drink.

A rather confused German businessman got up from his table and made his way over to Gillian Maclaine. He explained that there must be some mistake, as he was a reformed smoker, and had not touched a cigarette since the end of the war. Maclaine smiled and explained that he was merely repaying a debt, and went on to recount when the debt had been incurred. The gentleman, a Herr Bauer, shouted with surprise when he realized who he was talking to, and the two of them spent a convivial evening drinking and filling in the intervening years.

Serendipity is a wonderful thing.

September 2016

Ashes to Ashes

Ann Cumberland was a feisty old lady, of great intellect and with a sharp sense of humour. She lived in a neat cottage in Helderberg Village, a retirement village for the wealthy in Somerset West, close to Cape Town in South Africa.

She lived alone since her husband, Richard, had died some three years before, and she lived her life busily, playing bridge, travelling with old age groups, and attending concerts in the nearby town of Stellenbosch. Ann had a wide circle of friends, who all valued her friendship, and her two children, Mark and Deborah, held her in high esteem for her intelligence, her wicked humour and the love that she showed them at every opportunity.

Mark now lived in the UK with his wife and small son, but managed to visit his mother every year, and to fly her to England every second year. Deborah, who lived with her boyfriend, André, in Cape Town, saw her mother every weekend, and sometimes at a concert during the week.

Ann had been blessed with a robust constitution, and was seldom ill in any way at all. She refused to see a doctor unless in extremis, calling them all 'quacks and sangomas', and frequently said that the quickest way to get sick was to visit a doctor.

In August of 2010 Ann caught a bout of 'flu that was doing the rounds, and took herself to bed for a few days. Deborah visited her every second day, checked that she had enough medication and food, made her chicken soup, and generally did the 'good daughter' stuff. The old lady slowly recovered, but 'flu at the age of seventy should not be taken lightly, and Ann suddenly felt her mortality a little more.

Mark was due to visit at the end of September, and Ann decided that it was time to update her will and get her affairs in order. When Mark arrived—without his family this time—Ann asked that he and Deborah should visit her at lunchtime on a Saturday. She would order pizza for the three of them, and, accompanied by a bottle of Eikendal Sauvignon Blanc, they would go through the new will that she had drafted.

The day was a stunner, a preview of the summer to come, and the old lady was in high spirits: she had enjoyed her pizza, eaten three slices with gusto, and was now on her second glass of the refreshingly cold white wine.

"Right you two!" she addressed her offspring. "Not much has changed in my will, but as I have been enjoying life at your future expense, there isn't quite as much to go around."

The two young adults looked at her fondly, "Spend the lot, Mum," suggested Mark, and Deborah chimed in, "We don't expect anything anyway, and you will probably live to be a hundred, so there certainly won't be anything left by then."

"And you, young lady, will go and wash your mouth out with soapy water! A hundred indeed, how dare you wish such a fate on me!" Ann smiled and took their hands in hers. "No, I'm not going to make a hundred, but I would like to get everything straight with the two of you now."

"I want to be cremated," Ann continued, "and I would like to have my ashes scattered in the waters of the Steenbras Dam."

Her children nodded, and Deborah quietly said, "I'm not sure what the law says about the scattering of ashes in Cape Town's major water supply, but we'll get around it somehow."

Ann waved away the slight objection regally and carried on: "Your father and I loved it down next to the water there, and we often went there for a picnic at the weekend." She had a dreamy look in her eye as she continued, "Yes, both of you kids were actually conceived on a tartan rug next to the dam, after a bottle of wine and a damn good lunch!"

There was a disbelieving silence for a good few heartbeats, and then Mark, with his eyeballs on stalks, gasped, "Ma, you have got to be kidding!"

"No," was the rejoinder, "I never kid about good lunches or sex."

Ann beamed at her shocked offspring, and poured them all another glass of wine. Deborah slowly picked up her glass, was about to take a sip, when she stopped, raised it and quietly said, "To Dad." Mark pulled himself together and repeated the toast.

With the dreamy look still in her eye, Ann said, "To you, darling Richard, and to the fun we had." She started to giggle, and eventually burst into loud laughter. "You, Debs, nearly weren't conceived on the banks of the dam, your father got such a fright from a large puff-adder that he almost lost the urge!"

The old lady rocked with laughter as she recounted how a naked and virile Richard had suddenly spotted a movement near the edge of the rug; he had leapt up, tangled his feet and nearly fallen on top of the serpent! He eventually reached for a fallen branch and used it to move the somnolent snake away, so that it headed off along the bank of the dam.

Mark and Deborah hugged their mother and Mark promised to visit again the following day. They left at dusk, driving back to Cape Town together, as Mark was staying with André and Debs for this visit. That evening over dinner, Mark recounted to André the story of the snake on the banks of the dam, and they all had a good laugh.

The next morning Mark borrowed Deborah's car and drove out to Helderberg Village to see Ann. He arrived at the gate and was duly allowed in, courtesy of Deborah's pass on the windscreen. He drove carefully along the well-tended little roads to the cottage where Ann lived, and was surprised to see an ambulance parked on the verge.

With mounting concern, Mark jumped out of the car and ran inside. He was confronted by a gentleman carrying the front end of a stretcher, so he backed out of the front door to allow the team to carry the stretcher out. He saw immediately that there was a blanket over the face of the body, and realization hit him: Ann was dead.

It seemed that she had gone to bed, and had been looking through a photo album when she had quietly fallen asleep with the bedside light on, and had simply never woken up. She had been found by her cleaning lady, who had come in through the kitchen door, to which she had a key.

The album was open to a page of rather faded photographs showing a tartan rug on the banks of a dam or a river as a background to two photos, one a picture of a pretty woman wearing a bikini, and the other of a tall man wearing a pair of board shorts. They were good-looking people in their thirties, both smiling and happy.

The date, written in ball-point pen at the top of the page was 14th January 1978.

Mark had been born on 20th October 1978.

***

The arrangements for the funeral, the cremation, and the gathering for drinks afterwards was very efficiently done with the help of the village management—they had to do this quite a lot of course, as retirement villages are likely to have a higher death rate than most communities. By the end of a week, everything had been attended to, including the clearing of the cottage and the reading of the will.

Now came a problem.

Mark's family, languishing in London, wanted him home. He was determined that he would like to see through the whole catastrophe, and help with the scattering of his mother's ashes. André had ascertained the road to get them all to the Steenbras Dam, and the team of three decided to set off on the Thursday afternoon, deposit Ann's ashes, have a farewell dinner in Cape Town, and take Mark to the airport on Friday morning.

The best laid plans of mice and men …

At about two o'clock on the Thursday afternoon, the three piled into André's old Land Rover, and set off along the N2 towards Sir Lowry's Pass. The urn containing Ann's ashes was in a basket, along with a bottle of cold Eikendal wine wrapped in newspaper, and three glasses. It was a lovely day and the traffic was light, so they made good time, and just after three o'clock Mark spied the sign to Steenbras Dam. They turned to the right, and were immediately stopped by a boom across the road.

A little old man dressed in a Metro Police uniform approached the car and asked André what they wanted. André explained that they wished to visit the dam, which they could now see at the bottom of the hill. The old man shook his head, and explained that the dam was no longer open to the public—it was very dangerous. He kept repeating, "Baie gevaarlik!" When asked what was so dangerous, he said that the place was positively dripping in venomous serpents.

André looked at the two siblings, and said in English, "I'm sure that there is another route up from Gordon's Bay, let's try that." Mark and Deborah agreed, and, waving goodbye to the little uniformed gnome, they turned the Landy and set off back down the pass.

The drive through Gordon's Bay was as depressing as usual, covered as it was with some of the ugliest houses ever built. They followed the road towards Cape Slangkop and found the turn-off to Steenbras as they came out of Gordon's Bay. The road was steep and convoluted with a number of hairpin bends and, as they came around the last corner, they were confronted by another boom across the road.

"No," said a rather unfriendly character, "the road has been closed for at least four years, by the Cape Town Municipality."

The frustrated threesome parked the Land Rover, got out and sat on the wall overlooking False Bay. Mark was determined that his mother's wishes should be followed through, no matter how illegal it might be, and Deborah backed him up. André was a little more circumspect and pointed out that they would have to wait for dark before attempting any trespassing on municipal land.

They eventually drove down the hill into the rather shabby waterfront of Gordon's Bay, found a restaurant and sat outside under an umbrella to wait for the sun to go down. They ordered a bottle of wine and made their plans.

They agreed that the easier of the two entrances was the one at the top of Sir Lowry's Pass, where the water was a scant 200 metres from the road, and where they would quite easily slip through the wire fence and walk down to the water. The bottle of wine was finished so they ordered another, along with some nasty-looking fried calamari to soak up the alcohol.

By the time night fell, Mark and Deborah were fairly tight, with Deborah slightly teary and Mark in a rather 'gung-ho' mood, relishing the walk down to the dam. André, though he had drunk less than the other two, was also 'ticking' and was keen to get back on the road and get the job finished.

On arrival at the top of the pass, they realized that it was an incredibly dark night with no moon at all, and the stars, though bright, would not be much help on the walk down to the dam. They had found a torch in the Landy's cubbyhole, but the batteries were almost dead. They parked a short distance beyond the gate house, which was in darkness, but they were not keen to gamble on passing by unseen, preferring to brave the open scrub between the road and the water.

They pulled the strands of rusty barbed wire apart, and slipped through one after the other, talking in whispers and trying not to giggle. Mark had the basket with the ashes and the wine on his arm, and he held on to André's jacket with his free hand. Deborah, who was not wearing suitable shoes for a hike like this, was slipping and sliding, holding tight to André's hand.

The ground sloped a lot more steeply than they had thought, and the 'fynbos' clutched at their legs as they stumbled down the hillside. It was a good twenty minutes of walking that finally got them to the edge of the dam, and they were able to climb down onto the dried mud at the high-water line. The recent droughts had dropped the water by a good metre and they had to drop down quite steep bank to scatter the ashes.

André let out a despairing cry as he started to slide on the dried mud, which turned out to be not-so-dry under the surface. He grasped Deborah's hand tightly, and so dragged her down with him, shrieking all the way, and they both hit the water in a sitting position, coming to a stop in water up to their waists. Mark had sensibly let go of André's jacket, and was sitting on the upper bank shaking with helpless mirth. He suggested that they should wade along the edge of the dam towards a tree that seemed closer to the water, so that they could use the branches to pull themselves out.

This plan worked, and they all gathered under the branches, André and Deborah covered in black and greasy mud. They opened the screw top of the wine bottle, poured three glasses and toasted Ann. Deborah again burst into tears, while Mark wrestled with the lid of the urn, and André looked around nervously. "Did you hear something?" he whispered to Mark, but at that moment the lid suddenly flew off the urn and dropped into the water.

"Shit!" said Mark as he eased himself down to try and retrieve it. He held the now-open urn in his left hand, bent his knees and used his right hand to fish for the lid. As his feet slid out from under him, he fell head-first into the water, losing his grip on the urn, which immediately filled with water and sank.

At this point all three of the intrepid mourners started to see the idiocy of the situation. Mark lay in the chilly water and hooted with mirth, while André and Deborah held each other and cackled away. Eventually Mark managed to get out of the water, and they finished the bottle of Eikendal while they sat and shivered on the bank.

"Bye Ma, I'm not sure that this is what you had in mind, but I know you would have laughed," said Mark as he drained his glass.

The journey back to the car was not going to be easy, and so they started off in a line, with André breaking the trail. He suddenly stopped, and the other two bumped into him, "There's something there, right in front of me!" he whispered. Mark got the sick little torch out of the basket and shone it over André's shoulder.

There was a puff-adder, about three feet long, revoltingly puffed up (hence its name), and hissing. The three adventurers slowly backed up, and found a way around the beast, deciding that they were not interested in disputing the right of way with such a bad-tempered serpent.

André now used the torch every half minute or so, as he had a healthy terror of putting his foot down on something that would bite him. After about ten minutes, the torch gave up the ghost, and André started making a very nervous humming noise in his throat. Deborah developed verbal diarrhoea, and would not shut up, while Mark stayed silent, but kept looking behind him as though he was sure that someone or something was following him. It was while his head was turned that he lost his footing, wrenched his ankle, fell into the fynbos and started screaming, "It got me, it got me! Oh God! It bit me on the hand!"

André and Deborah, almost at the end of their tethers, whipped round and saw Mark thrashing around on the ground. André reacted first: he grabbed Mark and lifted him up, at which point Mark lifted his right hand to try and see what had caused him such pain: he was expecting to see a couple of puncture wounds from a snake bite, but instead (and to everyone's great relief) there was a sharp piece of wood sticking out of his palm. Deborah, who had suddenly sobered up and calmed down, gently removed the offending stake and tossed it away.

The large amount of noise that the party had made had attracted the attention of someone in the guard hut, and a torch beam started to quarter the area of bush. All three miscreants ducked down and stayed quiet, and soon the guard at the gate got bored and went back inside.

The rest of the trek took a while, slowed down by Mark's injured ankle, but was free of any more shrieks and alarms. They regained the Land Rover, and climbed gratefully into it, started up the engine and turned on the heater.

They were quiet on the return to Cape Town, and it was only as they turned into Gardens that Deborah broke the silence. "You know, all I can hear is Mum laughing herself insensible."

Mark chuckled, "Yes, the old girl must have nearly wet herself watching that debacle."

Avoiding the Black Cat

The year was 1999, and it was high summer in the Cape province of South Africa. Jim Selway was leaving his place of business in Montague Gardens to drive home to Somerset West where he lived with his wife Liz, and his eight-year-old son Carl. They lived in Somerset West, despite the long drive from Montague Gardens, because Liz had a florist shop in the town, and because there were good schools for Carl to attend.

Jim walked towards his car, rummaging in his pocket for the keys, when a large black cat streaked across in front of him. Jim leaped in the air and let out an oath, which was heard by his foreman who was also heading for his car.

"What's up Jim?" called the foreman, whose name was Dirk.

"A bloody great black cat just ran across in front of me, scared the hell out of me," mumbled Jim.

"Was it running from left to right or from right to left?" asked Dirk.

"From right to left, but what difference does it make?" Jim replied.

"Well, if it was from left to right, you have good luck coming, but if it was right to left, watch out, there's bad luck waiting for you."

Jim just shook his head at the inanity of the superstition, climbed into his car and readied himself for the long drive home in heavy traffic.

He eventually arrived home to his neat and solid house on Irene Avenue, and wearily walked up to the front door, keys at the ready, when the door was jerked open from inside. Liz stood there, her normally attractive mouth pursed up like a sour prune. "I want you to speak to your son, this very minute!" she said, and Jim immediately felt the tiredness in his bones crank up another notch.

"What has the little hooligan done this time?" he asked as he gave Liz a quick kiss and a squeeze. Without replying she took his hand and led him through the house to the sitting room, where a big French window looked out over a well-tended lawn. In the middle of one of the glass doors was a large and ugly hole.

Carl was summoned, and arrived in a cowed and miserable state. It transpired that he had been playing cricket in the garden with two friends from school, and had been batting when he had tried a pull-shot that he had seen played in the last test against Australia. He had connected all too well: the ball smashed through the glass, his two friends did a runner over the back fence, and his mother had descended on him like an avenging angel. She had confiscated the cricket bat and thrown the cricket ball (in a girly sort of way) out of the back door.

Jim was too tired to thrash his son, and anyway, he knew what it was like to be in trouble for similar incidents when he had been a boy. Liz later berated him for being 'soft' on Carl, to which he mumbled "Yeah, yeah," as he poured himself a well-earned scotch.

Night fell, dinner was eaten, dishes were cleared away into the dishwasher, and the family prepared for bed. Poor Jim fell asleep as his head touched the pillow, and he didn't move for the next few hours.

His sleep was disturbed at around two am by Liz. "Jim," she whispered, "Jim, wake up, there's someone in the garden." She accompanied this with a shake of his shoulder. With a mumbled "Whaat?" Jim surfaced groggily from the depths. Liz repeated herself, and Jim tried to concentrate. Now hearing the vague noises from the garden, he came fully awake very quickly.

He leapt out of bed, clad only in his boxer shorts, reached into the bedside table and grasped the 9mm automatic that was secreted there, cocked the pistol and silently made his way downstairs. There was a good moon, and so he crept towards the French windows in the sitting room, gently moving the curtains apart to see into the garden. There was nothing to be seen, but his field of view was restricted, and he was about to unlock and open the windows for a better look when he had an idea. Crouching slightly, he stuck his head out through the hole in the glass, to avoid forewarning an intruder by noisily opening the windows.

Jim swung his head left and right, but could see no one despite the bright moonlight. He was about to withdraw his head from the glass, when Shadrak, the Siamese cat, rubbed himself across the back of Jim's legs.

Jim's heart nearly stopped, and his immediate reaction was to try and stand upright. He sustained some very unpleasant and messy cuts to the back of his neck and his trigger finger reflexively tightened on the automatic. There was a huge bang, and a rather pretty porcelain lamp on a corner table exploded into the air.

Jim managed to get his head inside, liberally spraying the curtains and the beige carpet with his lifeblood, and sank to the floor whimpering loudly.

Liz, never short of courage, burst into the sitting room brandishing the confiscated cricket bat. "Where is he?" she screamed, "come out you bastard!" Jim managed to tell her that there was no one there, and begged her to call the ambulance. Liz dialled 10177 and quickly explained that her husband was bleeding badly, all over her beige carpet. She grabbed a roll of paper towel from the kitchen and rested Jim's head on it while she explained to a sleepy Carl what had happened, and sent him back to bed.

The ambulance arrived from Vergelegen Mediclinic, and the two medics quickly strapped up Jim's neck, draped his dressing gown around him, and walked him to the ambulance parked in the driveway. Liz tearfully waved her husband off, and went to examine the mess in the sitting room.

It was horrible.

In the cupboard under the sink she found a bottle of white spirit, poured some into a bowl, and collected a new roll of paper towel and a small sponge. She set to work.

The blood on the curtains came off pretty well, but the carpet was a different matter, and after an hour's work there were still obvious stains that were really obstinate. Sighing, Liz started back towards the kitchen to dispose of the cleaning equipment, when there was a heavy banging at the front door. Being careful, she quickly dumped the white spirit and the wad of used paper towel down the guest toilet, and then put her eye to the spy hole to see who was at the door.

There were two gentlemen in police uniform standing outside, so she opened the door and invited them in. "Ja mevrou," said the elderly white sergeant, "there is a report of a shot being fired in this area, do you know anything about it?" Liz explained what had happened, and the young black constable looked for the bullet hole in the wall behind where the lamp had stood.

The sergeant tried unsuccessfully to hide the amused smile on his face as Liz told the whole story. He bent down and picked up the automatic, removed the magazine, cleared the weapon, and sniffed the barrel. He handed the firearm back to Liz, advising her to put it somewhere safe, stated that he was satisfied with the account of what had happened, and he departed with his constable.

Liz went back to the kitchen and had just started washing out the bowl and the sponge, when there was another bang on the front door. She rushed back, again checked the spy hole, and saw her husband standing outside, supported by one of the medics. She opened the door and let him in, thanking the medic who headed back to the idling ambulance in the driveway.

Jim explained that he had needed only five stitches in his neck, and that Casualty was so busy, they had stitched him up and sent him home. He was looking pale and drawn, and said that his stomach was not right. He picked up his packet of Marlboro and a box of matches, went into the guest toilet, closed the door, took off his dressing gown, dropped his boxer shorts, sat down and put a cigarette between his lips. He struck a match, lit the cigarette and dropped the match into the pan.

The fumes from the white spirit ignited with a loud 'WHOOSH', and Jim let out a terrified shriek as his genitals and buttocks sustained serious scorching. He fell forward onto all fours, just as Liz, having heard his screams, slammed the door open to investigate. The door caught Jim on his left ear, leaving it bleeding and bruised, and the poor man sank onto his side, sobbing quietly.

Liz ran to the telephone and once again dialled 10177, by some chance connecting to the same operator who—although slightly confused by a request for another ambulance to the same address—routed the nearest one immediately. This happened to be the same one that had picked Jim up before.

The two medics surveyed the scene on arrival, and agreed that they would have to use a stretcher to get Jim to the ambulance, and that using the front door was not an option due to the sharp turn from the hallway. They gently laid Jim face down on the stretcher and carried him through the kitchen to the back door, which Liz held open. There were three steps down to the driveway, and it was necessary to turn the stretcher slightly to avoid the garage wall.

The medic at the back was just swinging his end of the stretcher over the handrail, when he put his foot on the cricket ball earlier thrown by Liz. With a despairing cry Jim was flung off the stretcher, falling to the asphalt below, where he dislocated his shoulder and broke his wrist. When he was again safely on the stretcher, the medics drove off once more to Vergelegen, where he spent the next two days … the doctor in Casualty was convinced it would be too dangerous to send him home, where further damage might ensue …

Always remember, left to right is fine, but right to left is bound to bring bad luck!

September 2016

Birds from Hell

I have a very real aversion to parrots, and vice versa: they dislike me. I suspect that this goes right back to my childhood, when my family lived in Venezuela.

My dad took me and my mother to the Angel Falls, the highest falls in the world. We flew there in a de Havilland Dove, a light twin-engine aircraft that my dad used to make his rounds of South America as Her Majesty's Air Attaché at the Caracas Embassy.

We were the first aircraft to land at a small bush strip, and it was all very exciting for a five-year-old. We slept in hammocks under reed thatch, were shown around by Indians with spikes through their noses, and stayed for three days. On leaving, we were showered with gifts: bows and arrows, blowpipes with wooden darts (all devoid of poison, I hasten to add) and a young Green Parakeet.

I stretched out my hand to said parakeet, who immediately ran up my arm and cuddled into my neck. I was entranced, and then the bloody bird bit my ear with incredible ferocity.

That was the end, I never even tried to be friendly to it again, and the moment its clipped wings had grown enough feathers, I left it out on the balcony of our house in Caracas with the cage door open. Good riddance.

Many years later I was living in South Africa, and I took up with a feisty Afrikaans girl called Elise. Elise had a menagerie at her cottage in Gardens, Cape Town, including four parrots in an aviary in the yard. The parrots were from every corner of the globe. Jackson was an African Grey with soul of pure evil, and he had a female consort whose name I have forgotten. Spike was an Australian cockatoo and was as badly behaved and as aggravatingly raucous as anyone or anything from that country. Charlie was a blue Macaw from the Amazon. His claim to fame was that he was the dumbest bird imaginable. She also had a delightful and intensely intelligent Border collie called Jet.

127

Jet and I shared a dislike of the birds, but we reserved our special hatred for Jackson and Spike. Charlie just wasn't worth the effort.

Jet liked to lie across the passageway in the centre of the cottage, where he would quietly sleep during the heat of the day. The parrots were out of their aviary a lot of the time, and would walk around as though they owned the place. Charlie would stay in the aviary though, as he suffered from severe paranoia, and always seemed on the verge of having a heart attack.

Spike, in typical Australian fashion, would destroy anything that he could get his huge beak around, including Jet's tail. There would be a yelp, followed by a snarling lunge, and the sound of Jet's claws scrabbling for purchase on the yellowwood floor, while Spike legged it for a chair high enough to keep him away from Jet's jaws. Spike ate everything: my favourite pair of Docksider shoes, the wooden strips between the windowpanes and even the telephone lines at the top of the telecommunications pole at the corner of the property. He was so destructive that eventually even Elise realised that he had to be restrained, and he was often locked up in the aviary with the mentally incompetent Charlie.

Jackson was, however, the original Bird from Hell. He would advance down the passageway, tapping his beak on the wooden floor, and saying "Come! Come! Jackson, come!" while spoiling for a fight with me. Jet would lift his lip and snarl, but then creep out of the way with his tail between his legs. If I tried to pass Jackson in the passage, I was guaranteed a bleeding ankle, followed by an evil chuckle from the revolting bird. His claim to fame was that he liked to dance to Country and Western music, his favourite track being 'Achy Breaky Heart', to which he knew all the words. He would become particularly excited by the long rebel yells. It was a sickening display.

Even Charlie wasn't safe from Jackson's cruelty. There were a few cats in the area, and they were fascinated by the birds. Elise tried to shoo them away whenever she saw them, but they always crept back. Jackson developed his own alarm signal whenever he saw one, and let out a loud 'miaou' to warn Elise that there was a cat in the yard. Charlie, of course, became almost catatonic with terror when there was a feline threat, and Jackson soon realised how much fun it was to go 'miaou'. He would wait until Charlie was almost asleep on his perch, then let loose a loud 'miaou', whereupon Charlie would let out a shriek and fall off his perch, sometimes concussing himself on the concrete two metres down. Jackson would then chuckle in his hideous manner and congratulate himself with a repeated "Jackson! Jackson!"

Elise was not really safe either. The dreadful bird would sit in her office, and take no notice of anything, until Elise decided to go onto the 'stoep' for a cigarette, at which point Jackson would let loose with a barrage of coughing noises, sounding like someone dying of emphysema. He could copy any noise, and one of his favourites was the squeak made by the rusty garden gate when it was opened. On hearing this noise, Jet would leap up and rush to the front of the house barking wildly at what he suspected was an uninvited intruder. On arriving and finding no one there, he would turn around and head back to wherever he had been sleeping, Jackson's scornful chuckles ringing in his ears.

My hatred of the birds eventually finished the relationship.

Years later I fell in love with another Afrikaans girl, Sune. Sune's stepfather died, and she was left a small green Amazonian parrot, very similar to the one that I had as a child. When Sune had her small coffee shop, the parrot resided there and there was no problem. On the odd occasion that she brought the bird home, it always made a lunge for me through the bars of its cage. Typical parrot aggression.

I eventually had to lay down the law: "The bird goes or I go!" Thank goodness, the bird went.

October 2014

Little Red Hooding Ride

One day, long ago in the wild forests of Kwa Zulu Natal, there lived a big bad wolf who rejoiced under the name of JZ.

JZ was a cowardly and foul creature, who always took what he wanted without paying for it and cared not at all about the poor people in his area. Yebo!!

JZ was passing a kraal near his home of Nkandla when he saw an old grandmother making putu outside her hut.

"Hau! Sanbonani Grandmother" shouted JZ the wolf, "may I eat of your putu?"

"Aikona! You no-good impisi," shouted Grandmother, "you always steal people's food. I am making this very special putu for my granddaughter, Little Red Hooding Ride, who is visiting me this afternoon on her way to the DA rally, so you go and beg food from some of your ANC cronies and leave a poor old grandmother alone!"

JZ the wolf gave a low growl and jumped onto the grandmother, ate all her putu, and then gobbled her up for good measure.

Later that day, Little Red Hooding Ride, carrying her bundle of DA election pamphlets, came to the kraal where her grandmother lived. She stooped and entered into Grandmother's hut, where she saw Grandmother lying under a kaross in the darkness.

"Eish! Grandmother, why is your head so funny shaped and bald? And why is there a shower sticking out of the top if it?" cried Little Red Hooding Ride.

"All the better to think and plan the elections with," said JZ the wolf, for it was he under the kaross.

"Eish! Grandmother, what big eyes you have!" exclaimed Little Red Hooding Ride.

"All the better to buka the wonderful ANC future, my child," answered the wolf while licking his large and swollen lips.

"Hau! Grandmother, what big teeth you have!" cried Little Red Hooding Ride, shifting her grip on the stack of DA pamphlets.

"All the better to eat you with, you tasty little piece of nyama!" shouted JZ as he leapt up from under the kaross.

But Little Red Hooding Ride was ready for him, and shayaed him around the head with the DA pamphlets, bending the shower and making him howl.

"Sala kahle JZ," said Little Red Hooding Ride as she left the wolf moaning on the ground. "Go and have your head seen to at your private clinic at Nkandla, and leave the world of politics to a real party – the Democratic Alliance!"

The moral of the story is that wolves should stay out of politics, grandmothers should learn when to keep quiet, and that bright young girls have everything going for them.

May 1999

Paddy, Rudy, Dave and Water

The Durban Aquarium had a marine research wing, the Oceanographic Research Institute. ORI employed quite a lot of young scientists, all of whom took their grants from varied organizations in order to fulfil their project aims. The young scientists were often strapped for cash, especially when it came to living expenses, so any free hand-outs were really welcome.

There were three fellows who were truly blessed: Dr. Campbell, one of the sponsors and supporters of the Aquarium, owned a beautiful tract of land, just north of the Umhlanga river. This was a small nature reserve, and it had two dwellings on it. Peace Cottage was the larger, and was empty; Meadowbanks was the smaller, a combination of three rondavels (round African huts) all joined together in a triangle. The covered area of the open side was used for cooking and a toilet, and each of the three huts was fitted with a bed and a cupboard.

Dr. Campbell offered Meadowbanks to ORI, as accommodation for struggling young scientists, so three lucky guys moved in. I will call them Paddy, Rudy and Dave. The outside shower was the only washing area, and was fed from a rain butt on the roof. The butt filled up every summer and somehow lasted the dry winters (maybe because the guys did not like showering in the cold).

One of the fellows was nearing the end of his thesis for his MSc and he was very chuffed when a professor of ichthyology, visiting from the UK, read and commented on his paper. He invited the 'prof' back to Meadowbanks for a drink one evening, and took the trouble to ask the prof's secretary what he liked to drink. The prof's tipple of choice was Ballantines Scotch, without ice, and preferably with pure stream water.

Lucky about the 'no ice' requirement: Meadowbanks possessed no fridge, icemaker or water other than the water in the rain butt.

The other two were given strict instructions on how to behave while the prof was there, and the plan was set in motion.

The prof arrived in Paddy's beach buggy, a little surprised that it was possible to hear a leopard so close to Durban, and that Paddy should need to warn him about the mamba that lived under the second rondavel.

Rudy and Dave had put their time to good use, and had grabbed a couple of 'crays' off the reef at the base of the sand dunes, and these were slowly roasting over a small fire.

The ensuing conversation went something like this:

"Professor, may we offer you a drink?"

The prof looked happy, and replied, "Do you have a scotch by any chance?"

To which the artful Paddy said, "I believe we have a bottle of Ballantines somewhere, is that alright?"

"Absolutely perfect, young man, my favourite scotch."

Rudy chimed in with, "Sir, would you like that with ice?"

"Certainly not!" replied the prof.

The plan was working like a dream.

"Do you have fresh water here?" the prof demanded.

"Unfortunately, sir, we have only rainwater from the butt on the roof," said Dave, pulling his weight in the scam.

"Magnificent!" cried the prof, "that could not be better."

The boys scurried around, poured his drink, opened beers for themselves, and attended to the lobsters on the fire.

The professor took a sip of his scotch. He frowned, and then asked to see the bottle.

Paddy looked worried and asked, "Is there a problem, sir?"

The prof shook his head, and just said that maybe the scotch tasted different in different countries.

He refused a second drink, and hardly touched his cray before asking to be driven back to his hotel in Durban.

Paddy drove off with him, while Rudy and Dave cleared up. They were both wondering why the prof did not seem to enjoy his scotch, and Rudy noticed that the glass was still a quarter full, so he took a sip.

"This tastes like shit!" was his comment.

The two of them worried over the problem, tried the scotch on its own, (which tasted alright) and then agreed that maybe they had noticed the odd strange smell when they showered, and a funny, oily look to the water when they occasionally made tea.

They got the ladder out from under the middle rondavel (being careful not to disturb the mamba) and, holding a torch, Rudy ventured aloft to look into the water butt.

Paddy arrived back at Meadowbanks just in time to witness Rudy puking his heart out from the top of the ladder.

There was, in the water butt and blown up to double its normal size, almost devoid of hair, and in a fairly advanced state of putrefaction, a large and very dead vervet monkey.

Paddy still got a good recommendation from the English professor, so the water clearly hadn't killed him …

Strandfontein Road

I have been back in South Africa for a wonderful twelve days. I have revelled in seeing all my friends again, in drinking great wines affordably, and in settling in again with my lovely and long-suffering Sune.

My bakkie has been serviced, I have again become accustomed to the fabulous vistas and the warm weather, and life is truly splendid.

My very good friend Paul is back from the Caribbean, and I caught up with him last week. We drank and ate, and his wife Caeleen picked some of their very tasty habanero chillies for me to take home.

I have to add these to my own portions of food, as Sune is a bit of a 'girl' when it comes to chillies. I chop them carefully, taking out all the seeds, and put them in a small bowl with some olive oil, so that I can add them to whatever I am eating. Given the choice, I would add them to everything from cornflakes to ice-cream, such is my passion for the fiery little devils.

My social life has been hectic: lunches in Franschhoek to visit Laurie and Irvin Brittan; an evening at Eikendal for wine and pizza with Ryno, Virginia and their small son Christian; an evening with our lovely friend Marci; my aforesaid visit to Paul and Caeleen; and Sune continues to fill my calendar with dates for dinners, drinks and lunches.

One old friend who I was determined to see was Rob Fridjhon, who I last saw in Antigua some twenty years ago. We have been speaking on the phone over the last few months, but I had not managed to get my timing right to actually see him. On Monday last I decided to drive over to Lakeside, where he is living, and pay him a visit.

My morning started well enough. I was vaguely domestic around the house after Sune had left for work, then replied to a few emails and caught up with the latest news (including the unfortunate loss of the Proteas to Australia, and the devastating loss of the Blitzbokke, also to Australia … isn't it time to put all those people back into shackles and chains?) Finally, I chopped up the last of the habaneros, left them to stew for the evening meal, and drove off in my disgraceful Mitsubishi bakkie.

I enjoy taking the Strandfontein Road along the coast of False Bay, where the surf always lines up so regularly and the white beach is littered with drying kelp, the odd lonely fisherman and swooping gulls. Unfortunately, one also has to drive past one of South Africa's horror shows: the shantytown of Khayelitsha, which seems to grow as you watch.

I had passed Khayelitsha and was speeding along past Mitchell's Plain when a 'muggie' (small bug or midge), flew past the side of my sunglasses and into my left eye. I swerved slightly and blinked rapidly to clear my vision as the road descended towards the beach. The bug refused to move, despite some fairly muscular contractions of my eyelid, so I ripped off the sunglasses and rubbed the eye.

With my left hand.

The hand that holds the chillies as I chop them.

I had merely rinsed the hand when I had finished, not scrubbed it like a surgeon before an operation, which is what is required to get rid of all traces of the virulent juice of a habanero.

At this point things got quite interesting. My bakkie was swerving all over the road, while I let out a keening cry and my eye started to water with real intent. It was like a small and reddened Niagara: the tears were literally spurting from the tortured organ.

I pulled over towards the sand at the side of the road, narrowly missing a dilapidated Toyota Cressida with about ten fishing rods sticking out of the window. The three gentlemen who were standing on the beach looking at the surf were now treated to a live show of some drama.

I skidded to a stop on the sandy verge and leaped out of my vehicle, all the while trying to wipe my eye with the back of my right wrist. I hopped around in a circle, still yelling, with my right arm bent in a peculiar manner—it is hardly surprising that all three fishermen took a few steps back and stared at me in alarm.

"Water!!!" I screamed, "please give me some water!"

The fishermen just carried on staring at me, and one muttered, "Die oom lyk kranksinnig, pasop!"

And totally deranged I must have looked, hopping around and sobbing. The three of them wasted no time in jumping back into their Cressida while uttering cries of "Fok! Pasop vir die mal ouk!" directed at the people on the beach as they high-tailed it off towards Muizenberg.

By now I had managed to grind the chilli juices into my eye, and the pain was really quite breath-taking. I had a sudden flash of brilliance and started to run down the beach towards the sea, passing the trek (dragnet) team who were launching their small boat. They scattered out of the way, as you would if confronted by a rabid pariah dog foaming at the mouth and howling.

I ran into the water, and stood there, knee-deep, desperately using my right hand to splash seawater into my left eye. By now my vocalising had descended to a sort of moaning sound, punctuated with exceptionally foul language.

A small wave broke over my knees just as I scooped another handful of water, and naturally I now managed to rub a few grains of sand into my eye, just to really finish the job. The treatment seemed to be working though, and the intolerable stinging subsided to an almost bearable pain. I now started to wash my hands, using the sea sand to scrub the fingers of my left hand, while splashing more water into the eye every half-minute or so.

I noticed there were a few interested onlookers just up the beach, and one of them, a large lady carrying a handful of plastic Pick 'n Pay bags in which she was hoping to carry fish caught by the trek-netters, seemed to speak for all of them.

"Het die oom van Valkenberg ontsnap?"

I tried, in my best Afrikaans, to set the poor lady's fears to rest, and I assured her that I was not an escaped inmate from the local mental hospital. She gave an expressive sniff, and informed me that if I was not a lunatic, then I certainly had no right to frighten people and had no excuse for using such disgusting language in front of a lady.

I apologised profusely and made my way back to my bakkie, surprised to find it still intact as I had left it open all this time. Maybe the local populace is wary of stealing from those who display signs of insanity.

I eventually made it to Rob's house, and we were able to rekindle our friendship. He is a very well-mannered and polite man, and made no mention of my strange appearance, weeping and reddened eye, and sandy legs. His dogs, however, seemed to relish the salt on my legs, and licked me constantly during my visit.

I now take a good deal more care with my post-chilli-chopping cleaning regime …

January 2016

The Beach Buggy

In 1986 I was running a very beautiful yacht called *Cherry Blossom* in Durban, South Africa. The boat was owned by a prominent Durban businessman who really appreciated pretty boats. She was a Farr 55, stretched to just under 60 feet, built of aluminium, and had been refitted to a remarkable degree. The boat had a proper cruising interior, a water-maker, a near-silent new BMW diesel motor, a completely silent generator, autopilot and a new suit of sails.

As a young yacht captain, I was incredibly proud of the boat, and my friend and 'mate', Charlie Cramer, felt the same. We laboured over the varnish-work below, the gleaming winches on deck and the cleanliness of the galley and interior.

We ran the yacht up to the Seychelles and kept it up there for six months, while the owner visited from time to time with his family or lent it to friends to use. On returning to Durban, we had a fair amount of work to carry out in order to bring the boat back up to scratch.

The owner had given us a company car to drive, and to use for 'ship's business'. It was a venerable and very sedate Peugeot 404 automatic which had belonged to his father, and it obviously had to be kept in first-class order. However, it was not the sort of car to use for transporting heavy (and sometimes greasy) spare parts, so Charlie and I were not disappointed when the boss told us that a gang of accountants, who were doing an audit, would be using the vehicle.

They had used it for only a week before it spontaneously caught fire one night, and burnt out on the side of the road. Needless to say, Charlie and I were extremely relieved that we had not had responsibility for the motorcar when the incident happened. Our reputation with cars was not the best.

We were then given the keys to a rather battered fibreglass beach buggy, which had resided under the offices of the owner's company in Morningside for years. Charlie and I turned up on a Tuesday afternoon, collected the key to said buggy, went down to the open garage and set about getting the old VW engine to start. Eventually, after much coaxing and the loan of a starter pack from a garage, the machine exploded into life. It backfired, ran, nearly died, then caught properly and ran sweetly. The buggy was open, and had no canvas top, and the whole interior was filled with dust and leaves, but it was decent transport and, to Charlie and me, a vastly preferred machine for our needs.

We jumped into the dusty interior, and set off back to the Yacht Club on the Esplanade, stopping along the way to fill the tank with petrol. We thought briefly of using a carwash, but decided that we could wash it ourselves back in the bay.

It was now nearing five o'clock in the afternoon on a hot spring day in Durban, and the traffic was hectic, so I chose to drive down to the beachfront, and then head up West Street before turning down Field Street towards the bay. Charlie and I were both dressed in our casual uniforms of khaki shorts and white golf shirts, now very grimy from the interior of the buggy.

I turned up West Street, and immediately the bright afternoon sun just about blinded me and, having no sunglasses to hand, I reached for the sun visor that was attached to the top of the windscreen, and flapped it down.

There was, and had obviously been for some time, a very large baboon spider on the top of the sun visor. Caught by the breeze caused by the car's forward motion, it flipped backwards towards me, falling down the front of my golf shirt.

Now I am not a great fan of spiders and, when they are extremely hairy and weigh in at about ten grams, I am even less enthusiastic about them. The fact that the beast had disappeared down inside my shirt was the last straw.

I shrieked in terror and turned the wheel towards the curb, mounted it (very nearly running over a grandmother with her small

140

granddaughter) and came to a halt halfway up the pavement. Charlie was also screaming, but mainly in terror of my execrable driving.

I was still yelling loudly as I leaped out of the buggy and ripped my shirt off. The huge (and probably very frightened) spider fell to the pavement, where I tried to stamp on it, failing miserably. It nimbly scuttled across the pavement and down into a stormwater drain. The grandmother took me to task about nearly killing her and her grandchild, and all I could do was stutter an apology, while pointing a shaky finger at the spot where the spider had disappeared. Charlie, meanwhile, had climbed out of the buggy and was eying it with great suspicion—how many more of the brutes might we find between and under the seats?

Needless to say, we searched very carefully before gingerly climbing back into the machine and setting off for the Yacht Club.

Funny, I was nervous of that buggy forever after …

October 2016

Things that Slither

I am not good with snakes. I am always the first one to see them, trip over them, and to be frightened halfway to death by them.

I had flown in to Durban to see old friends, and to spend time in a city that had been home for some ten years. I hired a car at the airport, and drove up to Kloof for a weekend with my cousin Lorne Maclaine and his wife Sandy: good food, great company, and a quiet, restful ambience.

On the Monday I drove down to the Natal South Coast in order to visit my old friend Charlie Cramer. This was never going to be a restful time. Charlie had recently married a local girl in Port Edward, and she did not seem to think that Charlie deserved to have any previous friends. Said previous friends certainly should not visit.

Charlie had recently built a 'spec' house in Port Edward, and was in the process of selling it. He shuddered theatrically as he described the size and number of the green mambas that he had to destroy when clearing the land. I am not sure whether my sleep in his house was disturbed on account of the stories, or because of the pins that I am sure his wife was sticking in a voodoo doll made for my benefit.

Charlie and I left the next morning and went to stay in a friendlier environment with our friends Dave and Deborah Thomas who also lived in Port Edward, and they welcomed us in.

The south coast of Natal in January can be extremely wet, and this January was no exception. It poured solidly for two days, and we spent them in bars and restaurants, catching up on years of news and lies. At the end of the second day, the local golf course was a lake, and Dave's garden was a large pond. By the next morning the rain had stopped, but the true horror of the situation was revealed.

When it rains that hard, everything that lives underground escapes to drier areas. As the waters receded, the whole district proved to positively dripping in venomous serpents. There were two on Dave's lawn, another on a bush at the entrance to the driveway and, horror of horrors, one disappearing under my car as I started to put my bags in the boot preparatory to driving back to Durban.

Now I do not subscribe to tales of snakes finding ways to enter cars from underneath, and even though I had left a passenger window open about an inch, even someone as 'slang geskrik' as myself cannot possibly believe that a snake can climb the smooth shell of a car side.

There was no snake under the car. There was no snake anywhere near the car. So where was the snake?

I procrastinated for a while, cleaning the inside of the windscreen with some paper towel, checking the oil and water, but eventually I had to get going.

The weather was muggy and hot, and the air conditioning system seemed short of gas—it would run for a while, then suddenly blow hot air into the car—so I switched it off and opened the driver's window. I reached the freeway, turned right for Durban and accelerated up to 140 kph. The further that I drove from Port Edward, the less I thought about the case of the disappearing snake.

I was wearing shorts and a pair of sandals because of the heat, and when something cold, rough, and terrifying touched me on the back of my left leg, I felt it with every single nerve ending in my body.

I screamed.

I steered for the shoulder, stood on the brakes, watched in horror as the car did a stately 360, and stopped off the road. I leaped out like a baboon on speed, almost before the car came to a standstill.

Whimpering with terror I confronted my attacker. A large, slightly damp bundle of paper towel had blown off the passenger seat, touched the back of my leg on its way to the floor of the car, and knocked about fifteen years off my life.

At this point the normal person laughs, gets back in the car, and continues the journey. I, however, spent a good half-hour searching the car from bow to stern: under the seats, in the boot, above the sun visors, in the tailpipe, under the bonnet and in every other nook and cranny I could find.

I eventually got back in and set off once more for Durban, praying that the missing serpent was indeed safely back in Port Edward ...

November 2001

PART THREE

BLOODY BOATS

A Bar in Barcelona

There is, in the 'barrio' of La Barceloneta, a delightful little bar on the Carrer de la Maquinista. It is called Paso de Agua, why I cannot imagine, as I have never seen anyone drinking water in there. It is owned and run by two young South Americans, Pablo comes from Colombia and Ramon comes from Venezuela, Both have an eye to the main chance, as I discovered when stopping in late one night for an ABF (Absolute Bloody Final) after a riotous dinner with old friends. I asked for a large Johnnie Walker Black Label on ice, was served with a smile and panache, and was then asked for fourteen euros as payment.

Fourteen euros! I explained to Ramón that he must have made a mistake, I wanted to pay for one drink, not pay off his mortgage for him. Realizing that I wasn't quite as drunk as I may have appeared, he smiled ingratiatingly and said that he had made a mistake, and that the bill was seven euros. I was delighted with myself, and made the mistake of reminding him of his 'mistake' on my next visit.

Sune came to visit me in Barcelona, and Paso de Agua was one of the many haunts that I took her to, to show her where and how I spent my off-duty hours. She was understandably confused by the state of the place—there is not a single matching chair or table, the two 'comfortable' upholstered chairs are in a dire state of repair, and I personally would cringe if asked to sit on them, as I am sure that they carry traces of everything from the Black Death to Ebola Fever in their filthy velvet coverings. Pablo was on duty the night that we stopped in there, and he studiously explained the make-up of the bill when he brought it. He had obviously been told by Ramón of my surprise when Ramón tried to rip me off.

There are a number of 'regulars' who frequent the bar, and many seem to be denizens of the 'barrio', which is an old and fairly poor part of old Barcelona, abutting the port and close to the beach. The

146

residents are a real mixture, comprised of young Spanish students, immigrants from all over Asia and Africa, and a high proportion of elderly pensioners. Some of these last are not just elderly, but decidedly decrepit. They speak very loudly to each other from a distance of only half a meter, they cough, hawk and spit with decades of practice at ridding themselves of the result of years of inhaling strong tobacco smoke, and they certainly don't give a damn what anyone thinks of them.

There are a couple of them that are under the impression that they have proprietary rights to certain chairs and tables in Paso de Agua, and they are perfectly capable of asking someone to move away if they wish to sit in said favorite chair. Pablo and Ramón are likely to back up this colonial attitude of their ancient but regular customers, usually with an apologetic smile and a shrug of the shoulders.

The other evening, a rainy and blustery one, I was happily ensconced in the bar, a large vino tinto in front of me, my Kindle on the table, and a Salsa Colombiana quietly wafting from the speakers behind the bar. I became aware of an unpleasant odour, and of a wheezing very close behind me. On turning around, I saw an ancient crone, dressed in an expensive overcoat and holding an umbrella in one hand. In the other hand was one of those sprung-coil leashes, on the other end of which was a particularly ugly little dog. It was a terrier cross of some sort, wearing a coat in the colours of Barcelona Football Club, snuffling and wheezing in a faithful parody of its owner, and it stank to high heaven.

The old lady mumbled something at me, which I neither heard nor understood, but in my best Spanish I asked her whether I could help her in some way. She repeated her original mumble, and I saw Pablo hurrying over. He asked me, very politely, to please move to another table, as this lady always sat where I was sitting. I looked around and saw that the only other vacant table was the next one along, so I smiled, picked up my drink and my Kindle, and moved. The old lady sat down in my seat, gave me a toothless smile (which explained the unintelligible speech), and Pablo came back and placed a glass of Cava on the table in front of her.

The small dog moved over towards me and lay down at my feet, where it farted with real menace. The smell was horrendous, and I wondered what on earth the old woman fed the brute, because this was not the gastric gas of a healthy animal. Just as this thought went through my brain, the old lady also broke wind, loudly, unashamedly, and going by her countenance, with great pleasure.

I was appalled. I still had at least half a glass of wine to drink, and here I was trapped in a miasma of sulphurous misery. I decided that the dog and its owner probably ate the same food, and I suddenly felt quite nauseous at the thought of their shared home. I glanced up at the bar, and to my chagrin, there was Pablo holding his sides with silent hilarity, the tears pouring down his face as he enjoyed my acute discomfort.

That was enough. I knocked back the rest of my Rioja and staggered to the door, just as the dog once more let fly. The door is a sliding glass panel, and in my rush to get out, I very nearly ripped it off its channel. A couple sitting near the door seemed to be looking at me with extreme distaste. Could it be that they suspected that I was the source of the malodourous cloud? I was past caring, and slipped out into the cold and wet cleanliness of the Barcelona night, where I took long, bracing breaths.

A French Fishing Boat

During the 1970s there was a very likeable scientist working at the Oceanographic Research Institute in Durban, named George Hughes.

George was a Scot, and rabidly proud of it. He had come to ORI from the Natal Parks Board, and was completing his PhD on sea turtles. In order to do the necessary research, he travelled extensively, from the long sandy beaches of Zululand to the island of Madagascar, and on to the Mascarene Islands of the South Indian Ocean.

George's pursuit and tagging of his beloved turtles didn't always go according to plan, and his mishaps provided good fodder for the birth of legends.

***

George had a tripod that could be erected over the nesting female, and then a webbing strop could be passed underneath the gravid beast while she dug the hole to bury her eggs. This was then attached to a chain block with a scale hooked to it. By lifting the exhausted turtle, her weight could be read, her measurements taken, and under her, the number of eggs in the nest could be counted.

George was going through this process on a beach somewhere between Sodwana Bay and Kosi Bay. He had reached the egg-counting stage, which takes some time (a loggerhead turtle will lay between 400 and 500 eggs), when one leg of the tripod slowly subsided into the sand, and 150kg of tired turtle slowly settled onto George's back, pushing him down into the sand.

Now this might not have been quite so serious if George had had an assistant with him, but these were few and far between, and sometimes there were none around willing to work for love alone. So, picture George with a turtle on his back, the tide starting to turn, his

Landrover slightly seaward of him on harder sand, and only the faint hope that a Parks Board ranger would happen across him before the tide reached the high-water mark.

These exercises always took place at night when the moon was either full or new, and on this occasion the moon was new, so the night was almost perfectly dark. Unless George could attract the attention of one of the ten human beings within the surrounding 200 square miles, he was not going to be around to collect his PhD.

His luck held, and he was discovered and rescued by one of the rangers from Sodwana Bay, but the story went into the files.

***

East of Madagascar is the island of Saint Brandon (or Cargados Carajos Shoals as the old Portuguese mariners called it in the 17th century), which belongs to Mauritius. George had permission from the Mauritian government to visit the islands, and found himself a berth on a filthy little French fishing boat, registered in Réunion.

Now George is not the best seaman, and his French is not of the quality to really understand what is being said to him, so the stage was set for some miscomprehensions of enormous proportions.

On sailing out of Réunion, George had shown great bravado, joining the captain in a number of large glasses of pastis, a drink that should not be trusted under any conditions. That night the sea started to kick up, and by morning it was running at a good 3m, the swells exploding against the starboard bow of the malodorous little vessel.

George was in extremis. He was incredibly sick, and everywhere he turned he found another disgusting smell to upset his delicate stomach further. In the close confines of the crew quarters, where he was berthed, the reek of garlic sausage and strong cheese was enough to blanch a Zulu. Out on deck and despite the bracing trade wind, diesel fumes and the ghosts of a million fish wafted around the superstructure.

The captain came to find him, and, using simple French and sign language, explained that lunch was being served. George weakly shook his head and then quickly leaned over the rail again, offering up a very small gift to Poseidon, as there was nothing left in his stomach.

About an hour later the captain reappeared. He was obviously very concerned with George's condition, as there were still another two days of passage time before they would arrive in Saint Brandon, and it seemed doubtful that George would survive if he carried on in the present manner. The captain was waving his arms about, and repeating the word 'medicament' over and again, and George realised he was being offered a sea-sick remedy. He nodded weakly, then turned back to the rail and retched dryly.

George suddenly felt a pulling at the waist of his shorts, and before he understood what was happening, he had been bent over the rail, his pants pulled down, and a typical French 'medicament' in the form of a 'suppositoire' had been pushed up his backside.

One can only imagine the indignity felt by someone of George's sensibilities, but he did admit that from that day on he has never felt even a twinge of 'mal de mer' when the sea gets rough.

He does, however, say that at the first roll of a ship his buttocks close with an angry snap.

August 2010

A Most Fortuitous Meeting

In December 1983 I was sailing down the Red Sea in a 50-foot steel ketch called 'Nyati'. Nyati is the Zulu word for 'buffalo', and although the boat was far too beautiful to be likened to a buffalo, she was extremely tough and agile, just like her bovine namesake.

The passage through the Red Sea was the beginning of a return to South Africa, where the owner of the yacht resided. I had taken delivery of the vessel during 1982, completed sea-trials off Durban, and then sailed up to the Seychelles, where the owner and his friends joined me for an extended period. The boat was based in the Seychelles for six months before the owner decided to move her to the Mediterranean for a season. The voyage north was fairly unremarkable in that the weather was as it should be, there were no problems with the working of the boat, the crew of three behaved properly and there were no pirate scares.

We stopped in Djibouti for two days, enjoying the treat of good French bread and cheese washed down with rough red 'pinard' at the Club Nautique. The only excitement occurred one evening when we were all invited for dinner on a large Italian yacht. The only girl amongst my crew was a glamourous Australian called Kaye Maxey, and we were convinced that the all-male Italian crew was desperate to entice her on board. In fact, it turned out that they were far more interested in Jim and Peter, my two young deckies.

All very surprising and a trifle embarrassing.

I dropped the crew off in Larnaca, where I slipped the boat and spruced her up for the summer season in the Med. I was joined by a girlfriend who was keen to spend the summer as stewardess on board, but alas, it was not to be, and she flew back to Israel from Corfu. I completed the circuit of the Middle Sea with the owner, sometimes with his family, sometimes with his mistress, which was a lesson in discretion and diplomacy.

In November I was back in Larnaca, preparing for the return voyage to the Seychelles, and I had found a young Irishman called Patrick (what else?) as crew for the trip. We passed through Suez, my blood boiling yet again at the demands for Marlboro cigarettes and other forms of 'baksheesh', headed south and readied for the expected strong southerly winds once past Port Sudan.

These never appeared, and after a great three days of running free, the wind dropped and I was able to crank up the great big 70hp Ford 'iron spinnaker'. We kept up a steady 8 knots down to just north of Perim Island, when there was a loud bang from under the cockpit. I stopped the engine immediately and crawled into the engine space, could see nothing amiss, and slithered further aft to the gearbox. At first glance there was nothing wrong, so I yelled up to Patrick to restart the motor; he did so, and only when he engaged the gear did I realise that the coupling was not turning, so the shear pin had broken.

I dived over the side to check that there was nothing on the propeller, and found the remains of some polyprop rope, and surmised that we had picked up a fish trap that had caused the extra strain on the shaft. I cleaned the strands of rope from the shaft and checked that the propeller turned freely. A quick search through my spares box turned up a couple of bolts that were minimally smaller in diameter than the broken shear pin. I inserted one of them, tightened the nut and started the motor.

The bolt broke as soon as I engaged the drive. It seemed that the torque was too much for the slim stainless-steel bolts. As I sat and pondered the problem, a light breeze rose from the south, which helped me make the decision to try and find a replacement shear pin.

I still had a couple of hundred miles to go towards Djibouti, and having to tack the whole way (including the straits of Bab-el-Mandeb) did not appeal to me. So, without further ado, we set the mainsail and a jib and turned the bows towards the north in the direction of Hodeidah in Yemen. I had stopped there before when working on a Djibouti-based coaster, and although I had never been ashore, I was sure that there would be a workshop where I could get a couple of shear pins made.

We spent that night on a comfortable broad reach, arriving off the entrance of the bay at around 1000, and tacked easily in the calm waters down towards the harbour. I tried calling the port authorities on Channel 16 without success—there was always a few moments silence before the rapid Arabic again flooded the airwaves—so I decided to just carry on and find a berth. There was an open bit of quay between two large dhows, and I was able to drop the main and glide the last fifty metres before letting fly the jib and drifting in to the quay. Patrick jumped up onto the dock and took the lines that I threw him, and there we were, safe and sound.

Oh! So wrong.

There was the sound of yelling, and two armed guards came hurtling down the dock, waving their Kalashnikovs in the air and shouting very unfriendly-sounding words in Arabic. Patrick, who was still on the dock, received the butt of an AK in the stomach, and was roughly forced back onto the deck of Nyati, while I tried my best to show that I meant no harm to anyone, certainly not our attackers. I repeatedly tried to explain my nationality, brandishing my passport in one hand, while refusing to actually hand it over to the larger and more vociferous of these two buffoons. Eventually the second guard was dispatched towards the large port building further into the port, near a number of medium-sized freighters that were alongside the quay of the commercial port.

Patrick and I sat on the cabin top in the sun and waited patiently while our khat-chewing sentinel kept his weapon trained on us.

About an hour later a Jeep rolled up and came to a stop next to Nyati. A young-looking Arab with stars on the epaulettes of his shirt climbed out and spoke to me in reasonable English. He asked why we had entered the port without permission, and I explained that I had tried repeatedly to gain permission, but that no one had replied to my transmissions. He grunted and asked what our business was in

154

Hodeidah, so I explained deferentially that I needed the services of a machine shop, and that it was really a very small and quick repair, and we could be out of his hair before sundown.

The young officer was not convinced, and spoke rapidly to the guard, who saluted and turned back to us with his weapon readied. The officer then said that he would go and talk to the port director to see what could be done.

We sat on the cabin roof for another hour, by which time my patience had well and truly run out. I stood up and headed for the companionway hatch, ignoring the shouts of the guard. I swung down into the saloon, grabbing two hats and three bottles of water before re-emerging and offering the guard one of the bottles. He yelled something and then motioned for me to throw the water to him, which I did. I sat down next to Patrick, gave him a hat and a bottle and explained that we would have to do something soon, as otherwise I feared that we could be held there for days.

A second guard appeared to relieve the original at around 1630, and I quietly told Patrick to stand up, stretch, and move towards the hatch. He did, and the new guard took very little notice. I then did the same, and joined Patrick in the saloon, where I explained what I wanted him to do. Patrick made a sandwich for us to gulp down and prepared himself for the proposed operation. The tide was as high as it would get, having lifted Nyati's deck to the same level as the quay, and I had noticed that the second freighter on the commercial quay had a Red Ensign flying at the stern. Now was the time to try our luck.

I put the remains of the shear pin in the pocket of my shorts, my British passport in the other pocket, and explained the timing to Patrick.

As part of the 'baksheesh' that I normally carried into the Suez Canal, there were always a couple of 'Playboy'-type magazines, as I had found the Egyptians to be greatly enamoured of this kind of 'smut'. I was hoping that the Yemenis would be equally smitten.

155

Patrick casually walked up towards the bow, sat down with his back to the rail, and started to peruse the magazine, starting with the centrefold. He made some appreciative noises and chuckled a couple of times. Sure enough, the guard was curious and moved a couple of steps so as to be able to look over Patrick's shoulder. Patrick played his part magnificently and turned his back slightly towards the stern, so that the guard also had to turn in order to continue feasting his eyes on the forbidden delights.

That was my cue; I quietly stepped over the rail and trotted silently up the quay towards the British ship that I had selected. As I approached the gangway, I saw another Yemeni guard—checked keffiyeh, Kalashnikov and all—at the base. I slowed and tried to see the officer or bosun on deck, as the ship was taking on cargo. There was a pink-cheeked young fellow just forward of the gangway, and I called out in English, asking to speak to the mate.

He immediately used his handheld radio and, within a minute, the mate arrived at the head of the gangway. I explained very quickly what was happening, and he invited me on board, brushing aside the Yemeni guard's objections. I was taken straight to the mess, where there were a couple of officers having a beer. The mate went to find the captain, while I was offered a beer by an older officer. I asked the name of the captain, and was told that it was Captain Pym: I could hardly believe my luck if it was Rodney Pym, he was an OP (an Old Pangbournian), probably three years my senior.

Rodney entered the mess, and I introduced myself, explained the situation and asked whether he could help me. Rodney turned to the older officer, who turned out to be the Chief Engineer, and lifted an eyebrow. The Chief did not hesitate, but called for his second and told him to take me to the workshop in the engine room and make up a few pins for me.

It took all of thirty minutes and the job was done: I had five shear pins made of high-tensile steel in my pocket. I returned to the mess, was offered another beer by Rodney, accepted it and drank his health, the health of the Queen, Pangbourne Nautical College and life in general.

I thanked everyone, slid down the gangway to the now-dusky dock, and casually made my way to Nyati. I saw that Patrick, God bless him, had got hold of a torch, and was still sitting in the same position with the guard craning over his shoulder.

The guard noticed me as I climbed back on board, and I mimed stretching my legs as he started to make a scene and shake his gun at me. He hesitated and then turned back to the magazine in Patrick's hand. I called to Patrick and told him all was well, and that I would fit a pin immediately. I went below, crawled into the engine space, fitted the pin, which was tight enough to need knocking home with a hammer, and that was it: we were good to go.

I asked Patrick whether the guard had taken a break for anything, and he said that the man had been too intrigued, so I suggested that he gave the man the magazine, which he did. The guard immediately rolled it up and secreted it inside his loose uniform shirt, looking around guiltily as he did so. I told Patrick what we would do next, and we waited for the guard to move away, maybe for a toilet break. Sure enough, half an hour later he walked off into the dark of the dock, presumably to use the latrine.

Patrick and I worked fast and loosed bow, stern and springs, allowing the gentle southerly wind to blow us off the dock towards the open bay. I set the jib and we were soon into the outer anchorage, with no sounds of rage or pursuit. Maybe the Yemenis were actually happy to have us just disappear! I started the engine, engaged the drive and listened happily to the water chuckling past the hull.

Thank you, Rodney Pym, you were a real saviour!

July 2015

A Very Confused Pig

I am 'boat-sitting' in Barcelona for the winter. It is not too taxing, the boat is a 25m Delta, a very light 'go-fast' built in Estonia, and owned by a Swede. The boat has the feel of a sea-going Ikea advertisement, probably because of the light-coloured interior and the fact that it is designed and owned by a Swede. And because my brain is very susceptible to interconnecting bits of useless information.

I am alone on the boat, which suits me fine, as I have purposely developed a curmudgeonly persona while living alone at my home in Puget-Théniers. I have daily contact with the crew of the boat behind, a pretty Feadship called Gladiator. The captain, Andy, his partner Josey, and the rest of the crew are very pleasant, in fact they have invited me over for Christmas lunch next week. The first officer is a young Kiwi called Brook, who seems to spend as much time either running or in the gym as he does working—he is a nice kid, but I do find the constant exercise a bit exhausting to watch.

Next to the boat that I am looking after (called, by the way, *Stina Kajsa*, and no, I have no idea what it means), is an American-owned and registered cruiser called *Tamaroa*. The owner is a cigar-smoking American of senior years. He is interesting, and I would bet that he is a retired smuggler of high-class weed. There are two ladies who look like educated Cuban courtesans and who visit him often, bringing with them a small white dog that wears a coat of a different colour on each visit. The boat is cleaned by a pretty young blonde Spanish girl called Cris. Cris comes from Bilbao in the north of Spain, and is so full of energy, and so permanently happy and smiling that I have christened her the 'kitten on Ketamine'—not, you understand, to her face.

So that accounts for all of my neighbours, except, of course, Marcello. Now Marcello, who looks after a boat two moorings down, is an Italian/Spaniard, married to a French lady, and I am convinced he is on the run from somewhere or someone. He is so terribly careful when he gets off the boat, looking up and down the dock as though searching for danger. If you walk up behind him and tap him on the shoulder, he nearly has a baby on the spot, so yes, he is definitely suspect.

The other day I was busy in the salon, ordering bits and pieces from the dock agency, when Cris, the kitten on Ketamine, shot past the stern, shouting for me to join her. I made my dignified way onto the dock, and she was literally jumping up and down, pointing and trying hard to think of a word in English. She kept repeating "salvaje cerdo" (wild pig). Out in the middle of the marina, there were two inflatable tenders, criss-crossing back and forth, while the crew tried to throw bits of rope over something in the water.

Unbelievably, there was a big wild boar swimming across the harbour. He was not just staying afloat, but was swimming at a pace that amazed me, with a big bow wave coming off his shoulders.

He swam straight towards where Cris and I were standing on the cross-dock, which is on piles, and he then swam under it, cutting off the inflatables. They roared round to the other side, where Mr. Pig now appeared, and they tried to lasso him again and again—very poor efforts they were too. Eventually the boar ended up in a corner of the floating jetty, where he was finally caught.

The port police had been called, and were standing around smoking. When asked how they were going to remove the creature from the water they did the Spanish thing: they shrugged their shoulders. At last they called the fire department, who sent along a couple of fellows with a net, and the beast was removed from the water.

What on earth was a wild boar doing swimming around the marina? He can't have walked through the streets of Barcelona, so he could only have come from the sea, perhaps he came down the river to the east, then trotted along the beach.

I understood that he would be returned to the hills from whence he had come, but there was a gleam in the eye of one of the firemen that did not bode well for the pig's longevity … Christmas is just around the corner after all!

Just in case you think that the whole thing was merely a hallucination due to over-imbibing Rioja, here's my proof:

December 2017

An Awkward Owner gets his Just Desserts

The year was 1999, and the boat was a five-year old Broward named *Circe*. She was around 110 feet, and not in the best state of repair. The new owner, Mr. Garnish, had got himself a real 'deal' as the original owner had just gone to prison for some nefarious property shenanigans in South Florida, and Mr. Garnish was now looking to really enjoy his new acquisition.

Circe was berthed at Hall of Fame Marina in Fort Lauderdale, and a new crew took over on the Thursday. The captain was a young Australian by the name of Roger, and this was his first command, having recently passed his Class 4 ticket. The engineer was a morose and spavined Scot who never smiled before midday, but was a talented and innovative mechanic, and for some unknown reason had a deadly fascination for the opposite sex. There was a Puerto Rican deckhand called Miguel (a cheerful and totally inept seaman), and a chef from Louisiana named Darleen, who had an over-healthy appetite for beer and young men.

The last crew member hired was a stewardess, twenty years old, a vision of tumbling blonde hair, huge blue eyes, and a body to make a bishop sin repeatedly. Her name was Michelle, and she came from Quebec in Canada. The fact that she was totally and insanely in love with Bruce, the Scottish engineer, was beyond all understanding and belief, but she was; and she was also a very efficient stew, despite her tender years.

Roger had put the crew together on a frantic Wednesday morning, having been interviewed by Mr. Garnish at the Quarterdeck Restaurant on the Tuesday, and being told in no uncertain terms to get the crew on board before the weekend. Thursday and Friday were spent storing, cleaning and preparing for the arrival of the owner.

On the Saturday morning the crew were given a taste of how their lives would run for the period of their contracts on board: Mr. Garnish (whose given name was a rejoiceful Randolph) arrived on the dock with a 'heavy' who was not introduced, and a tired-looking Miami-Cuban beauty introduced as Señorita Morales. Garnish called the crew to the aft deck, and told them that he would look after them 'real good' as long as everything went his way, otherwise he would 'fire their asses'.

Super.

Garnish then said, without drawing breath, "Get me a jug of Margaritas, some ribs in BBQ sauce, and take me somewhere that boats like this go."

While the food and beverage department was doing its thing, Roger diffidently asked how long Mr. Garnish would be on board, as a precursor to deciding where to go.

"I will decide how long I'm gonna stay when I see how the Margaritas taste," said Garnish, trying to look savage.

"Right on," mumbled the 'heavy'.

Roger eased the boat away from the quay, praying to the (usually capricious) gods of seafarers to allow him to avoid any serious screw-ups.

Everything went fine until Miguel, trying hard to look 'cool' as he coiled the dock lines, stepped backwards off the deck, and landed on the swim platform with a sickening thud. Señorita Morales shrieked with laughter, Michelle screamed with fright, and Roger, turning to see what had happened, caught the last boat on the dock a glancing blow.

Why is it that whenever another boat is hit, it is either made of steel, or else has just had a new paint job?

This one was steel.

The irate Mr. Garnish struggled up to the fly bridge, where a shaken captain was trying to get control of the ship, while using the radio to communicate with Michelle, who was trying to staunch a bleeding wound in Miguel's head.

"What the hell you doing? You scared the s--t out of me, punk!" screamed the owner, dribbling BBQ sauce down his three chins.

Roger made placating noises, and steered the boat under the 17th Street bridge, heading for the port entrance.

By the time *Circe* exited the port, control had been regained. Miguel was sporting a dashing bandage around his head, the blood had been washed off the swim platform, and Mr. G was half-trashed on Margaritas. Señorita Morales and the 'heavy' had disappeared down to a guest cabin, not to have illicit and savage sex (as Michelle suspected) but to share numerous lines of cocaine while the boss slept and dribbled in the sun.

The sea was not kind that day, and soon the Señorita and the 'heavy' were back on deck, looking a little green as the boat rolled heavily on her southerly course, heading for the Keys.

Mr. Garnish woke up mean. He lifted his head from the cushion on the fly bridge, and growled, "What kind of asshole captain are you? I'm trying to have a good day with my friends, and you are making them sick." With that, he leaned forward and vomited copiously onto the deck. "Get the bitch to clean that up," he ordered, then leaned back and ordered Roger to turn and head for home.

Nothing loath—and trying to work out how quickly he could leave the boat—Roger turned the boat around and headed for Fort Lauderdale, while he called Michelle to clean up the deck.

Two hours later, *Circe* was back under the 17th Street bridge, Miguel and Bruce were preparing the dock lines, and Mr. G had recovered, thanks to the calm water.

When the boat was safely back at the dock, engines killed, shore power connected, and while the chef and stewardess ran up and down feeding the guests and pouring drinks for them, Roger started to relax a bit.

Silly fellow.

At about 20h00, Mr. Garnish yelled for the captain to join him on the fly bridge. Roger arrived, keen and eager.

163

"Fire up this mother," ordered the owner, pointing at the Jacuzzi. Roger tried to explain in diplomatic terms that the Jacuzzi needed work, and that the technician would only be on board on the following Wednesday. A vein started to pulse in Garnish's head, and he grated, "You're fired! Get your sorry ass off my boat!"

Roger felt a sort of lightness in his spirit and, ever the professional, he gave a small nod, removed himself to the lower deck and started packing his gear.

Mr. Garnish now called for Miguel, and told him to switch the Jacuzzi on. Miguel had no idea where to start, and so he was fired too, but ordered to stay on board until the arrival of a new captain.

By now, Bruce had realised that this was a no-win situation, and was getting his belongings together, with the idea of leaving that same night.

Señorita Morales ordered the cook to prepare some fried chicken, did not like the taste, and threw it all over the side. This prompted Darleen to call her 'Latino trailer trash'. Darleen was promptly fired.

The 'heavy' and Mr. Garnish had, between them, found the breakers for the Jacuzzi, ripped off the electrical tape that covered them, and switched the machine on.

The next few minutes were very confusing for all concerned.

The crew had congregated on the dock alongside *Circe*, waiting for Roger to join them and tell them what to do. Mr. Garnish, the Señorita and the 'heavy' were on the fly bridge, drinking and yelling insults down at the party on the dock.

Mr. G stood, stripped the clothing from his eminently unattractive body, and stepped into the Jacuzzi.

Now, the reason that the pool was out of commission, and that the switches were taped over, was that there was an electrical short of seismic proportions in the system.

The effect on Mr. Garnish was miraculous. His fat and flaccid body took on new tone and grace as he flipped backwards off the fly bridge, bounced off the rail on the main deck, and landed on the dock in front of the former crew, where he flopped around like a landed fish.

Bruce was first to recover, and he raced below decks to get Roger and the defibrillator from the medical kit. Michelle ran up to the fly bridge, where Señorita Morales was shrieking with hysteria, and the 'heavy' had passed out, having put his hand into the Jacuzzi.

Michelle slapped the hysterical Cuban as hard as she could, and was slapped back for her trouble, so she just left and rejoined Miguel on the dock.

Bruce and Roger jumped down with the defibrillator, ripped it open, and placed the pads on Mr. G's chest, while he quivered and let out keening little cries.

When the unit recognised an irregular heartbeat, it counted down and then gave Garnish a good jolt. He howled in terror and tried to get to his feet, but was restrained by Bruce.

The crew eventually walked off down the dock, leaving behind them a vitriolic stream of curses and dire warnings of legal action issuing from Garnish and Morales.

They had the last laugh: courtesy of the boat's credit card, they enjoyed a good steak at Chuck's (to get the bad taste out of their mouths) and took themselves to the Radisson for the night.

May 2013

Baudouse Cay

The distance is about 2500 miles from Mahé to Durban, and it could often be a boisterous voyage, but *Cherry Blossom* was a thing of beauty, seaworthiness and speed—a Farr 55 built in South Africa as a racing boat, then turned into a cruiser by Stan Donner—and we were looking forward to the trip. The crew was a motley crowd: my friend Charlie Cramer, our buddy Guy Gertrude, a young itinerant American called Jeff and myself as skipper.

We sailed from Port Victoria late one afternoon in February, and headed north of Mahé, turning west when we cleared North Point. My own personal sailing directions for this voyage, tried and tested, went like this: "Leave Mahé to port, head west towards the big island (Africa), after two days turn south. Stay in the current for ten days, then turn right for Durban. If your butter turns hard, you have gone too far."

The problem was that Stan had asked me to come down in February, cyclone season in the Mozambique Channel, so none of the usual rules applied.

By midnight we were reaching hard down the west coast of Mahé in a strong northwesterly wind, squall after squall sweeping through, sailing under double-reefed mainsail and a number 3 genoa, and making a steady 8 knots. Charlie and I went forward to check the reefing cringle on the gooseneck, leaving young Jeff at the wheel and Guy babysitting him.

The seas were bursting up onto the weather rail, lovely warm tropical water, so we were all dressed in baggies and T-shirts, nothing that gave protection of any sort … especially from flying fish.

Now the average flying fish weighs about twenty grams, but there are some species that grow much bigger, and the one that leaped on board that night was a monster, around three-quarters of a kilo. I suspect that it was a bit confused by all the lightning, because it flew high above the guard rails, accelerated through the belly of the mainsail, and shot between the spokes of the wheel.

It immolated itself when it hit Jeff right in the nuts. Jeff let out a groaning shriek and collapsed to the cockpit floor. He lay there like a dead man while the rest of us tried to stop laughing. In hindsight, he could have been quite badly injured by a fish that size, but besides sore balls and a liberal covering of slime he was fine. The fish did not fare so well, it left one eye mashed into Jeff's shorts, and then stove its head in on the cockpit seat.

We sailed on south for another three days in the same sort of weather, and then heard on my daily schedule with Mahé radio that there was a cyclone brewing to the south and east of us. I put a call through to Stan, the owner, on the SSB, and told him that we were going to turn back for Mahé and try again in about a month, after cyclone season.

We romped back to Port Victoria, taking the Cerf Island passage, and licked our wounds tied up to Hodoul Island.

Six weeks later the season had changed, and the southeast trade winds started to blow. It was time to try and head south again, so we stored up, filled up with water and looked for a replacement for Jeff, who had decided to fly out. We found a taciturn German called Bernd who wanted to get down to South Africa to buy some spares for his own boat. This time the weather was kind, and we had a wonderful wind on the port quarter all the way down to the Amirantes.

Guy, being a typical Seychellois, loved fishing, so he was all for it when I suggested anchoring for a night off Baudouse Cay. Baudouse is a very small uninhabited island on the western side of the Amirante banks, and was one of the few islands in the entire group that I had never seen.

We anchored off at sundown and had a peaceful night, leaping up at dawn to go and explore. Charlie and I went to look for lobsters, Bernd took a walk on the island, and Guy took the tender and decimated the reef fish in the area.

167

Charlie and I were swimming around, having no luck with lobsters, and had started heading towards the small beach where Guy had dropped Bernd, when we sensed that we were not alone. Relatively small reef sharks are not normally anything other than curious, but the one that was following us was either very bad-tempered or terminally insane.

I am not proud of the fact that I stopped looking behind me and just swam my butt off to get to the beach. It is my theory that you do not have to swim faster than the shark, just faster than your buddy. I was still getting my fins off when Charlie made a beach-landing like a ski boat, with five feet of whitetip reef shark biting his fins. Charlie did not say a word for about ten minutes, but the dark looks that he threw my way were eloquent.

The island is home to thousands of boobies, probably the most brainless of all our feathered friends. We came across one that had a broken wing, and was emaciated. Neither Charlie nor I are hunters, and catching and killing a fish is a very different proposition to putting a booby out of its misery. We eventually got hold of the bird, and then started arguing about who was going to have to wring its neck, and also how this was done. It was a particularly harrowing passage of time, and you can call me a wimp, but I would not like to repeat it.

Guy came to pick us up from the beach, and Oh, surprise! there was hardly room for us in the tender. It was filled to the sponsons with a heaving mass of snapper, rock cod and coral trout. I pointed out to Guy that we could never eat that much fish, to which he replied that we could freeze it, dry it, curry and bottle it, but we were not going to waste a single morsel. We ate only fish for the next fifteen days. Mr Donner had fish to last him a month after our arrival. Bernd did not even eat fish.

The good weather lasted all the way down to a point 200 miles south of the Comoro Islands, when the wind turned south and increased to about 35 knots, the sea started to get up, and within ten hours it was big, ugly, and very uncomfortable. We beat into the growing sea for the next two days, but our 'Distance Made Good' was very little, and on the evening of the third day we decided to have a rest. We hove to on port tack, under a triple-reefed mainsail, with the wheel lashed over to starboard. The boat was riding well, we were getting some rest, we had hundreds of miles of sea room and all was well.

Almost.

We had only two packs of cigarettes left and, as socially unacceptable as it might seem today, Guy, Charlie and I all enjoyed smoking. We saw a northbound freighter on the horizon the next day, and were so desperate for cigarettes that we actually tried to call it on the VHF, but either they didn't bother with a radio watch, or else they were just very anti-smoking, because they didn't answer.

The wind stayed constant in strength and direction for the next four days, and our relative comfort was only disturbed by Charlie fumigating the cockpit with a home-built pipe, stoked up with tea leaves. It was quite the most revolting-smelling smoke, Charlie was sick, and Guy and I almost swore off smoking for life.

Eventually the wind dropped a bit in strength and went back to the east; we set full plain sail and headed south, found the Mozambique current and flew along. The current gets stronger as it gets further south, and by the time we passed Maputo two and a half days later, we were getting 5 knots extra. The wind backed to the northeast, we set a three-quarter ounce tri-radial spinnaker and bowled along doing close to 15 knots over the ground.

Charlie woke me up at about five the next morning, looking worried and telling me that we had just passed a freighter inshore of us, which did seem weird—the ship must have been out of the current, and we were flying.

We made it into Durban before the yacht club pub closed that evening, and they sold cigarettes.

A happy ending to a magic trip.

June 2010

169

Big Ship, Little Ship

In 1981, I worked for a year at Mainstay Sailing Academy in Durban. The school was owned and run by a larger-than-life character who shall remain nameless. Suffice to say that he was as unbending as the masts of his yachts, was an inspiration to generations of would-be yachtsman, and is sadly missed since he passed on into the Great Blue Ocean upstairs.

I was put in charge of the long-range projects, taking students to Mauritius and the Comoros, usually so that they could complete their Yachtmaster Ocean qualifications. The head instructor at the time was Garth Hitchins, a very good racing skipper, born and bred in Durban. Garth told me a story about two of the students he had taught from day one.

They were a retired couple, fit and capable, and let's call them the Joneses. They had joined the school and had spent months working their way through the various courses, from the basic Deckhand course through to Coastal Skipper. Mr. Jones went on to complete his Yachtmaster Offshore. The idea behind this year of study and exams was that they wanted to buy a small cruising yacht, and set off round the world—a very attainable dream for people unencumbered by children, pets, or limited imagination.

The Joneses eventually found and bought a Morgan 31, very close in design to a Nicholson 31, seaworthy and safe, and an easy boat for the two of them to manage. They took their time preparing the boat for serious long-distance cruising, and I believe Garth was extremely helpful in giving advice and generally steering them in the safest directions.

They moved onto the boat and lived in Durban harbour, while daily practising all the new skills that they had learned. They also had the chance to befriend and get to know visiting cruisers, who were able to stiffen some of their ideas and give them food for thought.

170

They eventually set sail for Cape Town, 800 miles to the southwest, as dangerous a voyage as most cruising yachtsmen ever have to make. There are only three safe harbours where a yacht can find shelter between Durban and Cape Agulhas, a distance of 600 miles, and the weather is very difficult to forecast with any degree of accuracy.

Mrs. Jones was not yet very confident standing watches on her own at night so, on the way to East London (300 miles to the south), Mr. Jones stood all the night watches, and his wife shared the daylight stints with him. They had fairly boisterous northeast winds that sent them bowling along, helped by the Agulhas Current, and they made East London in sixty-five hours, despite having been very conservative with the amount of sail used. Here they stayed for four days, fine-tuning some of the systems on the boat, sitting out a strong southwest gale that came through, and feeling pretty pleased with themselves. On the fifth day the forecast was good, and so they set sail for Port Elizabeth, another 250 miles to the southwest.

Once again Mrs. Jones did not stand night watches, but she stayed up with her husband for some of his, and was gaining confidence at every hour. They reached Port Elizabeth without incident, and were feeling pretty 'salty' as they walked into the Algoa Bay Yacht Club, had their showers, and retired to the bar to discuss the trip with the members.

The care with which Mr. Jones watched the weather really paid off, and when they left for Mossel Bay (a small port 180 miles to the west), they once again had comfortable and safe conditions.

On this trip, Mrs. Jones decided she was ready to stand her night watches. On the first night out, she had the midnight to 04h00 watch in perfect weather and under a waning moon which stopped the night being quite so dark. Mrs. Jones felt perfectly content. At about 02h00 she turned around and looked behind her for the first time.

She shrieked in terror, bringing Mr. Jones up the companionway in a rush. Bursting onto the deck, he saw what had terrified his wife so.

171

There seemed to be an entire floating city bearing down on them from astern.

Mr. Jones had very good marks for his VHF radio licence and, under normal circumstances, was extremely careful to use only the correct radio language. At this point, however, all his careful study was forgotten as he grabbed the microphone and howled, "BIG SHIP BIG SHIP, THIS IS LITTLE SHIP, PLEASE DON'T HIT US!!"

He was rewarded with the following reply, in a very calm, very English voice:

"Little ship, little ship, this is big ship QE2. Please maintain your course and remain calm. We have had you on radar for the last 20 miles. We will pass you at 3 miles, and we wish you a pleasant watch. QE2 out."

Mr. and Mrs. Jones recounted the story to Garth, and suggested that more emphasis in lectures was put on a truly ALL-round lookout.

January 2010

Cape Town Radio

My friend Garless Grey was the senior operator at Cape Town Radio, probably the busiest marine radio station in the southern hemisphere. It was 1972, and shortwave radio was the only way that ships could keep in touch with owners, port authorities and loved ones.

Most ships allowed crew a certain number of radio-telephone calls to their families each month. To do this, the ship's radio officer would take down the crew member's home telephone details, then call the coast station with the best reception and book the call. The coast radio station would then call the ship back when the connection had been made, and the crew member would be put on the line to speak to Mom, Dad, girlfriend, wife or whoever. These calls were not private, and could be heard by anyone on the same listening frequency, although maritime law was supposed to prevent this.

A class of ship that spent more time than most others at sea, was the Japanese long-line fishing boat. Around 150 feet long, they carried a crew of about twenty-five, and when they wanted to call home from the South Atlantic, at least ten would want collect calls home to Japan, and Cape Town radio was the coast station used. Because of the language difficulties when the radio operator spoke to the ship, and ensuing language problems contacting the Japanese telephone operator and the crew member's eventual party, one can only imagine the mix-ups and high blood pressure that followed.

On a particular Saturday evening in November, Garless was on duty, and expecting a busy shift. He was not going to be disappointed.

A call came in from a Japanese fishing boat, "Cape Town Ladio, Cape Town Ladio, this Johalla Maru, Johalla Maru. You read me?"

Garless was onto the call immediately, "Johalla Maru this is Cape Town Radio. Johalla Maru this is Cape Town Radio. Receiving you Strength Five. How may I help you this evening?"

The excited voice came back, "Cape Town Ladio, This Johalla Maru, we want make telephone call Japan."

Garless, following procedure, said, "Johalla Maru, please go down to the working frequency and stand by."

The Japanese operator confirmed his understanding, "Cape Town Ladio, Johalla Maru, we go working frequency and stand by."

Garless now transmitted on the calling frequency, "All ships, all ships, this is Cape Town Radio. Is there any urgent traffic before I go back to the working frequency, as I will be off air for a while?"

A German ship came back immediately, saying that the first officer's wife was having a baby in Hamburg, and he wanted to check on progress. Garless did his best, but conditions were not very good and it was twenty minutes before he managed to get the German officer connected with his wife, a very tired new mother. The call went on for a good twenty-five minutes, and just before it ended, there was an excited squeal on the same frequency.

"Cape Town Ladio, Cape Town Ladio, this Johalla Maru."

Garless was on it like a shot, and he was quite short with the Japanese.

"Johalla Maru this is Cape Town Radio. Please do as you are told, and stand by. You are now turn number two."

The reply was most unexpected: "Cape Town Ladio, this Johalla Maru. I not turn number two. I sinking!"

The poor little fellow had hit a floating container while waiting for his call, and had been trying forever to contact Garless on the calling frequency. The crew were rescued by a nearby container ship, and all was well, but Garless said he was never short with anyone again on air.

Charlie's Shark

I was employed by a fellow called Stan Donner, who had bought a very beautiful racing yacht, *Cherry Blossom*. She was a 55-foot sloop designed by Bruce Farr. Stan had had her 'civilised', and put a proper interior in her. The decision was made to sail her up to the Seychelles from Durban, and let Stan enjoy the islands for a season.

I put together a crew of five: myself, a girlfriend called Tanja, Diana Runge who was a sailing instructor from Durban, and Dave Yoxall, a friend that I had worked and dived with for years. I also signed on a recently qualified Coastal Skipper called Charlie Cramer.

We left Durban in April, and headed north towards the Mozambique channel. The weather was kind to us, and we made good time up the Zululand coast, stopping for nearly half a day to watch a humpback whale and her calf. The calf came so close that the mother almost rubbed up against us to stay between the boat and her offspring.

Three days later we were in a patch of absolute calm on the east side of the channel. The water lay like glass, and the yacht was as still as if she had been on dry land.

The Mozambique channel is littered with tiny islands and reefs, and in those days of 'pure sailing', using only a sextant and a compass, it was a very dangerous place—knowing your position was everything. We were, to my best 'guesstimate', about 100 miles off the coast of Madagascar, and in 1500 fathoms of water.

Charlie (this was his first long voyage) asked if he could go for a swim, and of course I said, "Yes." He then asked if it was ok to dive off the bow, and asked whether there were any sharks around.

Well, of course I said he could swim where he wanted. As for the sharks, we would be watching out for him, and anyway you could see 300 feet in any direction in the crystal-clear water beneath.

I know it was cruel, unfair and savage, but we were young. The moment Charlie dived off the bow, Dave and I slid into the water from

175

the stern. We swam under the keel, came up under Charlie and gripped his legs with our arms.

Charlie stopped breathing. He trod water to such effect that he came out of the water to his groin. Dave and I helped him back to the swim platform at the stern; he still couldn't speak, and he lay there like a wet fish going into cardiac arrest. The result was nearly more than we had hoped for. It took three days before Charlie was willing to talk to us again.

We arrived in the Seychelles after a pretty uneventful trip. Di Runge and Dave flew home to South Africa, and the three of us settled into an idyllic lifestyle in Mahé. A couple of weeks later Tanja left for Switzerland, and Charlie and I were told by the boss that he had some friends coming to sail around with us for their honeymoon.

The couple duly arrived, and Guy Gertrude, a great Seychellois friend, joined us as deckhand. We took the newlyweds to Praslin, and then on to Curieuse Island to see the tortoises and do some snorkelling. While there, Charlie asked about spinnaker flying, and we decided to rig it up as an entertainment for the guests.

We put a strop on the anchor, and tied it off at the stern, so the bow was pointing downwind, and brought the ¾ ounce spinnaker on deck. The wind was about 10 knots, absolutely perfect, and Charlie was keen to take the first ride. Guy and I rigged two sheets through snatch blocks to control the sail, and we tied a line across the clews of the sail for Charlie to sit on. All was ready; Charlie sat on the pulpit, hanging onto the lines, and Guy and I sent the sail up on the halyard.

At about this point everything started to come unglued: the wind increased to about 25 knots, the halyard jammed with the sail only halfway up, the control lines shot out of the snatch blocks, and Charlie was whisked up to heights that were truly terrifying.

To compound the debacle, the anchor started dragging, and *Cherry Blossom* headed towards the reef. The bride started crying, her husband looked at me as though I had done it all on purpose and, to cap it all, Charlie started howling in (understandable) terror. I yelled at Guy to take the knot out of the bitter end, and let the halyard fly.

It was spectacular.

Charlie shot across the bay for about 25 yards, and came down in a bundle of sail and lines—thank God he missed the edge of the reef, because there was only a foot of water over the coral.

Guy picked Charlie up with the dinghy, and we put everything away in subdued silence. I reset the anchor, while the bride fussed over Charlie's scrapes and scratches.

Funny, but Charlie never asked about spinnaker flying again.

May 2009

Snoring – or Not?

Snoring is described as, and I quote, "the vibration of respiratory structures and the resulting sound due to obstructed air movement during breathing while sleeping."

Well, that is a mouthful for the sort of quiet noises that a spouse or lover might make on the odd occasion when a little too much red wine has been imbibed.

Researchers go on to say that snoring could be the first sign of OSA, or Obstructive Sleep Apnoea, which, sidestepping the medical claptrap, means that you may forget to breathe when asleep, and never wake up again.

Total and utter bullshit.

Do you know that researchers in the UK were paid over £4 million, over a period of two years, to try and discover what effect snoring had on the British GDP?

WHAT??

That meant that people were paid to listen to the moans from overcompensated housewives about the noise that their underworked men made when they went to sleep. Unbelievable.

I have been accused sometimes, by the girl that I love, of snoring. This is a base and groundless distortion of the truth, as I know very well that hardworking men NEVER snore.

There is a subtle and seditious feminist plot to accuse men of snoring, thereby to fill them with guilt and much distress. "My darling, I am so sorry, I never meant to disturb your sleep!" accompanied by much wringing of hands, visits to the chemist for miracle cures and, always, the guilt.

This ploy has been used by women down through the ages; I am certain that it was the cause of Helen's infidelity with Paris. I can just hear her saying, "Oh! How Menelaus snores at night, I have no rest. Please, oh beautiful Paris, take me away with you!" And a month later, she would be moaning at Paris, "But now you too snore like a pig! I shall not be able to sleep unless you buy me that amber bracelet in the market."

Poor King Arthur would have been accused of snoring, and that would have been enough for Guinevere to shack up with Lancelot. Lancelot would have been told that his snoring had destroyed the relationship, and the poor man entered a priory.

And here is the secret. Women have discovered that guilt over their lost sleep is the way into a man's wallet. The poor boob will buy her perfume, jewellery, a new car, in fact just about anything to assuage his guilt. I have a nasty, sneaking suspicion that girls learn all about this at their mother's knee.

"Now listen carefully my child, and you will always have a weapon with which to bring a man to his knees. Tell him that he snores, and that he makes life unbearable for you, and I promise you that he will be putty in your hands!"

I have just spent a delightful ten days on a yacht, travelling between Sharm el Sheikh in Egypt, and the Maldives. On boarding, I discovered that I would be sharing a cabin with my very good friend John Mason, who had supplied the security detail for the trip. John gave me an apologetic grin and said that he would like to beg my pardon in advance for the snoring that he was sure would wreck my off-duty hours. He told me this because his adorable wife, Anni, had told him that he snored impossibly. I cheerfully responded by saying that Sune insists on wearing earplugs when we share a bed, as otherwise my snoring keeps her awake.

Well, the truth is now out.

NEITHER JOHN, NOR I, SNORE AT ALL!!

During the entire voyage, with crossed watches (meaning that we each had to enter the cabin and go to sleep while the other was already asleep in their bunk) neither of us heard the hint of a snore from the other.

It seems that our respective partners have been using the age-old female method of receiving sympathy, and God knows what else, by playing on our guilt. Well ladies, we are now free men, we KNOW that we do not snore, and that any complaints of noise in the night are either imagined, constructed, or downright libellous!

March 2016

Stewardess Swims

When docking in a tricky position, it is often very helpful to have a crew member ashore to handle lines.

We were in Bermuda, anchored in St. George's, and had arranged to take fuel from a truck at a small jetty on the western side of the bay. *Royal Secret* was a 100-foot cutter, twin engines, bow thruster, and a joy to drive. There was a stiff breeze blowing across the bay, so I sent our stewardess/chef, Lou, across in the crew tender. Lou had been sailing since the age of five, and in fact first crewed for me aged twelve, so she had a world of experience.

Lou moored the tender and scrambled up onto the dilapidated concrete dock. I briefed the rest of the crew as to how this was going to work. Work it did, like clockwork…to start with… Ben dropped the anchor in plenty of time, and I reversed in boldly to try and negate the wind on the beam. At exactly the right moment Richard tossed the port stern line to Lou on the dock, and she took a good handful of it to drag to the bollard.

At which point things started to go wrong very quickly.

Unfortunately, Richard was not watching when he hit the button on the hydraulic winch, and he wrenched Lou clean into the water. Lou had very sensibly let go of the line, and was swimming clear, while I nudged the boat ahead with both engines. As the line sprang back to the boat, I managed to get it around both propellers. Ben had not heard what was going on aft, so he happily let out more chain as *Royal Secret* swung round head to wind.

I screamed and cursed.

Eventually Ben stopped easing chain, Lou swam to the tender and came back to the boat like a drowned cat, Richard looked suitably embarrassed, and I just fumed. We dived on the propellers and freed the line, lifted the anchor and started again.

By the time we were safely moored to the dock, the Bermudan truck driver had got bored and disappeared with our diesel.

The best laid plans, etc. etc.

***

A Bridge too Far

In 1990, I was skipper on a very pretty motor yacht called *Greybeard*, jointly owned by Mr. Padda Kuttel and Mr. Louis Shill, and proudly carrying the South African flag.

We were meeting Mr. Shill and a party of his friends in St. Maarten, and had entered into the lagoon prior to tying up at Palapa Marina. We had a few days' work to do, but were able to have a couple of evenings out to remind the crew that they were humans and not robots.

Mr. Shill arrived on time, and was in quite a hurry to leave for St. Barts, so we prepared to get under way in time to catch the next bridge opening.

Now, the old bridge at St. Maarten was quite a contraption; I do not remember the exact dimensions, but I think that a beam of 11 metres was the maximum that it could accommodate. We had been in and out a good few times on *Greybeard*, and we had plenty of space, but you still had to watch out for the current.

On picking up the anchor, we managed to also pick up the anchor of the sail boat next to us, then, having helped them relay their anchor, the wind pushed us across their cable, and I picked it up again, only this time with the port propeller.

The Aussie skipper on the sailboat was heard to mutter, 'Did I do something to this bastard's wife in another life?' I had no reply, and I felt for him.

Eventually we were out in the lagoon, and heading for the bridge. At only 3 knots I did not need to use the steering, just the throttles.

We lined up behind a couple of other boats and waited for the bridge to open, backing down all the while to negate the outgoing tide, which must have been up to about 2 knots.

The bridge opened, and we were off. I kept the speed up a bit so that I would have good rudder effect with the tide behind us, and headed for the bridge.

I pushed the electronic tiller over to starboard, and absolutely nothing happened. I was about to bring it back to amidships and try again, when the rudders started to move to starboard—and then would not stop.

In only a mild panic, I switched on the bow thruster and tried to oppose the rudders with the thruster. This was only partially successful, so the panic level increased.

I was already committed to the bridge, and my trusty engineer, Paul, had already organised the crew with fenders to try and lessen any damage that I might do, so we sashayed out striking the bridge only once, while Sune, the stewardess shrieked, 'John, stop the boat!' What? We eventually got through, anchored in Simpson Bay, and sorted out the problem: no fluid in the system...not the best way to impress an owner on his first voyage with a new skipper.

***

La Digue

My favourite island in the Seychelles is definitely La Digue. In the eighties, there were still no motor cars or bikes on the island, and there was no airstrip either. Guests for the hotels were picked up at La Passe, the port, by ox wagon, and they walked next to the cart that carried their baggage. One could rent bicycles, but that was it.

I used to visit the island quite often, anchoring either outside the little harbour wall, or else coming inside when there was room, dropping an anchor, and tying the stern to a coconut palm on the beach. Both positions entailed use of the tender, and both positions had pluses and minuses.

When the trade winds dropped, the heat built up inside the harbour, and the mosquitoes came and feasted on you every night, while outside there was often a ground swell running, which could make you roll alarmingly if the wind dropped. Sometimes you win, sometimes you lose.

I had come in this particular day with the owner and his family, and I had anchored outside. The swell was rolling in, so I had decided to find rooms for Stan and his family at Gregoire's Island Lodge. My big Seychellois friend, Guy, was with me, and he brought the owner's family ashore, while I went and arranged rooms for them.

It was about six o'clock in the evening and, by the time the family was settled, it was dinner time, so Stan invited Guy and me to stay for dinner. We had a typical Seychellois meal: a curry, some wonderful fresh fish, and a fruit dessert.

Guy and I said our goodbyes at around nine o'clock, and walked back down the sand road towards the harbour. The sand was white, as soft as talcum powder, and it puffed up between our toes. There was a full moon, and the soft sigh of the trade winds in the tops of the very tall coconut palms lining the road.

A sudden rustling in the treetops heralded the fall of a huge, heavy and dangerous coconut, which landed with a loud thud no more than a metre in front of me.

I looked at it, then at Guy, and I asked him if people were ever killed by falling coconuts.

His reply said it all: "No John, people are never hurt by them, but sometimes tourists are," he replied in absolute seriousness.

***

African Banks

I had been in the Seychelles for six months on my yacht, *Jaho*. She was a Tahiti Ketch, designed by John Hanna, and built in 1932. I loved the old boat dearly, but knew that I could not afford to keep her.

There are two very small islets at the northern tip of the Amirantes called African Banks, and I was very keen to visit them. I had agreed to sell *Jaho*, but the money had yet to come through. I decided to take a quiet, solitary sail to the banks for a couple of days.

I left Mahé, and sailed down Cerf Island passage, and out into the wide blue that separates the Seychelles granitic group from the Amirantes. The wind was a gentle southeasterly trade wind, and my course took me close to some potentially dangerous reefs, so I needed my wits about me.

Around lunchtime, I decided that I needed some sustenance, but was a little concerned that the fluky direction of the wind would take me too close to the outlying reefs. I relied on a very effective self-steering mechanism, which kept the boat on a constant course relative to the wind. The problem was that if the wind direction changed by 20 degrees, so did the course sailed, and at the end of the winter in these parts, the trade winds could easily veer back and forth by 20 degrees.

To keep a check on the course while I prepared lunch, I set up the small hand bearing compass as a 'tell-tale' on the chart table, and glanced across at it every so often.

I was chopping some makings for a salad in the tiny galley and noticed that a beam of sunlight came through the porthole and shone directly onto the chopping board. I checked the compass—dead on course—and I had a revelation: while the sunlight was on the chopping board, I would have nothing to worry about until the sun had moved across the sky a good distance.

At that moment, I honestly believe that I was the happiest man in the world. I poured a glass of wine, put a cassette of Jimmy Buffet's music on the little tape player, and settled down in the cockpit for a wonderful sail down to African Banks. It was idyllic.

The sea being the sea, the trip back to Mahé four days later was appalling, and I truly thought that I might lose the boat at one point. But I have never forgotten that wonderful afternoon and the sunbeam on the chopping board.

October 2010

Trawler Mary Kate

Koos Delport was a very fine trawlerman. He had fished out of Durban for twenty-five years, first as a lad on his father's boat, and then as share-holding mate on a bigger boat. He finally had enough money saved to buy his own vessel, the 56-foot steel trawler called the *Mary Kate*.

She was a modern little vessel, very strong and, for 1973, a fishing boat at the cutting edge of technical advancement. Koos had a Mauritian engineer called Vincent, and the two of them had sailed together, drunk together and whored together all over the southern Indian Ocean. The rest of the crew were Zulu, a huge bosun called Erasmus, and seven hands who were cowed and beaten by Erasmus on a regular basis. Koos spoke impeccable Zulu, and was respected and trusted by the Zulu crew, but it was Erasmus who was feared and obeyed.

The *Mary Kate* was a 'lucky' boat, and the crew were always getting bonuses for bringing in jackpot hauls of crayfish or prawns, depending on the season, and Koos had paid off the marine mortgage in double-quick time.

One weekend in April, the best prawn fishing month of the year, the crew were all given the weekend to go home, while captain and engineer prepared the boat for a survey. The crew were told to be back at work on the Monday evening, on pain of dismissal if they were late, as Koos wanted to sail for the Tugela prawn grounds on Monday night.

The survey passed without a hitch, and the crew dribbled on board in various states of inebriation, some of them sporting bandages on heads or arms. It had been a memorable weekend. By 20h30, when Koos wanted to sail, there was still no sign of Erasmus, and Koos decided to sail without him, appointing the leading hand, Tshabalala, as relief bosun.

187

The voyage went well, with six tons of prawns netted and frozen, and three days later the *Mary Kate* steamed into Durban harbour, docking at the fishing jetty on Maydon Channel.

Erasmus was waiting on the dock, looking a bit sheepish, but hardly apologetic, and Koos took no notice of him as he stepped ashore. Tshabalala grunted an insult at Erasmus, and the crew all roared with laughter. Erasmus seethed and spoke back to them in a voice heavy with menace.

It was now that Koos made a mistake that would cost him dearly in months to come, he turned to Erasmus and said, "Fuck off Erasmus, you don't work for me any longer; here is your back pay. Now go, and leave my crew alone."

The crew roared again, and Erasmus took a step back as though he had been struck, he looked at Koos through slitted eyes and said something under his breath before turning away and walking proudly down the dock.

Tshabalala looked worried, and turned to Koos, "Kahle baas," he said, "be careful, his father is a big sangoma near Kwambonambi, and he will put a tagathi on you." Koos replied that he was an 'umlungu', a white man, and he was not frightened of spells cast by Zulu witch doctors.

Three days later the *Mary Kate* was again ready for sea, and slipped out past Durban Bluff, heading north towards the Tugela. Within two hours there was a mechanical problem, and the reliable and well-maintained Mercedes diesel was overheating badly. Vincent stopped the motor and tried to find the problem. There was no cooling water coming through from the sea chest, so Vincent went over the side with a mask.

When he surfaced, he hauled himself on board and explained that there was nothing he could see in the intake, so the blockage must be in the short length of pipe in the engine room, but that there was no way to fix it at sea. By running the motor for fifteen minutes at a time, at very low revolutions, they eventually got back to Durban. The next day they plugged the intake, replaced the pipe, and all was well. They sailed on the tide.

This time they made it up to the Tugela Banks, shot the trawl net and trawled for six hours. When Koos tried to engage the hydraulic winch to haul in the net, there was a screeching sound and then nothing. The hydraulic pump had died, and there was no spare on board. With a heavy heart Koos loosed the pelican hooks holding the bitter ends of the trawl cables, having buoyed them in the hope of later recovery.

It was a very quiet and unhappy little fishing boat that steamed back to Durban. The fuel costs were great, the crew had only their basic pay, and Koos was eating into his savings.

A new hydraulic pump was fitted, fuel tanks filled, and off they went again, with a very expensive and brand-new trawl net and gear. This time all went well—they netted over 10 tons of prawns, found that someone had picked up their lost net, and then headed back to Durban.

On the way into harbour, Vincent was horrified to see that the temperature in the hold freezer was climbing fast and, by the time they were alongside, the prawn had all thawed. The buyer shook his head, and said that he could not accept the prawns. No one wanted them, and the only solution was to go back out to sea, at least 3 miles offshore, and dump the lot.

By the time they had finished and docked in Durban again, it was daylight, and Tshabalala came into the wheelhouse asking for Koos. He explained that the crew were unhappy and frightened, and that they all wanted to leave the boat before there was a real disaster. He said he was sorry, but that this thing was stronger than Koos, and it would eventually kill them all.

Koos climbed into his old pick-up truck on the Friday evening, and drove north towards Zululand. He arrived in Nongoma at about midnight, and slept in the truck until dawn. He had been given the name of a well-respected sangoma by one of the departing crew, and he had come to find him. He enquired at a couple of kraals, and eventually was given directions to the old man's home.

The sangoma, named Makhathini, lived with his six wives, numerous children, and a healthy number of fat red cattle. He received Koos with great dignity, and they sat and discussed the weather, the climate and other insignificant things while the old man's youngest wife brought them 'tshwala' beer to drink.

Eventually Koos broached the subject of why he was there, and explained what it was that he required. They agreed on a price—the cost of two cows—and the old man gathered the herbs, bones and other impedimenta that he might need. The unlikely pair then got into the pick-up and headed for Durban.

The sangoma was fascinated with the hustle and bustle around the port of Durban. He had visited it once before, he said, when the 'big war across the sea' started, so he must have been a young man at the beginning of the Second World War.

Koos helped the old boy over the rail onto the *Mary Kate*'s decks, and Makhathini immediately started hawking and spitting, saying that there was the smell of evil. He crept into the wheelhouse, and then down into the accommodation, flicking his wildebeest-tail switch, and sniffing the beams and lockers. He paused at the galley table, pulled some bones from his sack, and threw them onto the table, gasping in shock when he examined the fall. He hurried on deck, and then informed Koos that the 'muti' was too strong for him to cure, and that he was going back to Nongoma immediately, and that there was no charge for his services. Koos sadly took the old fellow to the bus station and bought his ticket, waving him on his way.

The next week, Koos and Vincent took the *Mary Kate* out on sea trials. They had gone over every part of the boat, and decided that as it was so calm, they would take the boat out and test everything. They had no need for crew, and left the dock at 10h00, sailing due east off the coast.

At 14h00, a fishing boat returning from the Tugela received a call from the *Mary Kate*, asking them to come and stand by, as Koos had some problems with a water intake.

At 16h30, the Mary Kate sank in 1500 fathoms of water; Koos and Vincent were rescued by the fishing boat standing by.

The official enquiry agreed that the eventual fate of the vessel was 'sinking due to misadventure'. Koos collected the insurance money, and started looking for another boat.

I met Koos in the Riviera bar a few months later; he was in his cups, and owlishly told me what had happened.

"Fuck, man, I had to go back twice and knock the sea cocks off with a sledgehammer, the bitch just wouldn't sink!"

It is what the industry calls a 'cash sale'... ka-ching!

January 1999

Unwelcome Visitor

Sotogrande was a really welcome port. We had just sailed *Royal Secret* up from Port Said in filthy December weather—the Mediterranean can be foul in winter—tough going even for a big, strong 100-foot cutter. The port is situated very close to the Spanish border with Gibraltar, so we had come some 2000 miles from Egypt: cold, missing the tropics, and longing for rest.

We spent the first night in port doing the usual: out on the town, catching up with old friends, drinking and eating too much, and enjoying a full night's sleep.

In the early hours of the morning I was awakened by the persistent sound of the freshwater pump. This was wrong. The pump only ran when there was a tap opened and the pressure dropped in the line. I climbed out of my warm bunk and set off to discover the reason, cursing under my breath at whoever had left a tap open. I stepped down into the galley area, straight into an inch of cold water.

I stopped trying to be quiet and yelled loudly enough for Richard, the engineer, to wake up and come to investigate.

We turned off the water pump and tried to find the source of the flood, which seemed to come from behind the washing machine.

After an hour's carpentry and swearing we moved the washing machine, to find that the water hose had been abraded … or was it gnawed?

The next morning, we examined it more closely, and decided that there were definitely tooth marks on the hose, and this pointed to there being a stow-away on board. A nasty, grey, furry and deceitful stow-away.

I went into town and bought a new water hose for the washing machine, and also a mousetrap, small to medium size. That night we set said trap with the requisite piece of cheddar cheese, and all went off to our bunks.

In the morning we discovered a number of interesting facts:

1. The trap was too small.
2. The rat had a high degree of intelligence.
3. It was also trained in first aid procedures.

The trap had been flung quite a distance, and we surmised that the rat had put his paw on the cheese, caught it in the too-small trap, and flung it off in rage. His next stop had been into the first aid kit in a galley cupboard, where he had helped himself to:

1. an Elastoplast, and
2. a Stopain

(and there was a bandage unrolled half round the galley).

At this point I declared total war, went off to the shops again, and returned with large rat traps, of the type that make your fingers squirm just to look at them. Richard was decidedly caustic in his remarks, "It's only a small mouse for Christ's sake, aren't you overdoing it?" But I was determined. That night we set two traps, and I swear that none of the crew slept a wink.

In the early hours there was a loud 'snap' and we all congregated in the galley. Guy was giggling and pointing at a large brown rat of at least a kilo weight that was dead in the trap. Richard just said, "That's not my mouse."

Me? I was just happy to be rid of the freeloader.

When Hunger Strikes

One of South Africa's foremost canoeists during the '70s was a young Natalian called Tim Biggs. Tim and his brother won the Duzi Canoe Marathon time and again; they were also great runners, and did the Comrades Marathon often.

I was on my Tahiti ketch *Jaho*, moored in Richards Bay—the port in Zululand—having attempted to leave for the Seychelles two weeks previously, but having been beaten back to port by a strong northeasterly wind. My one crew member (who also happened to be my wife) had done a 'stem head leap' as soon as dry land came within leaping distance, and was now walking inland carrying an oar, and waiting to be asked what that strange implement was. I was preparing to leave on my own, when an elderly man accompanied by a callow youth banged on the hatch.

Mr. Biggs introduced himself, and asked whether I was looking for crew. He seemed surprised that I had not heard of the callow youth, his son Tim. I explained that I knew little about canoes or the people who paddled them, and told him that I was very keen to find someone to help me sail to the Seychelles. The upshot was that Tim accompanied me to the Seychelles, a voyage that took twenty-seven days, a longer trip than usual, due to a combination of light winds and a very slow old boat.

I should explain at this point that Tim had some strange ideas. He was very proud that he was a fourth-generation vegetarian, not for religious reasons or for health reasons, but simply because his father's family thought it wrong to kill animals and eat their flesh. This humane but strict self-imposed diet included non-consumption of all meat, poultry and fish … just great on a yacht in the Indian Ocean. For the sake of his sport, Tim was also a non-smoker, and never imbibed alcohol.

You can imagine how surprised I was when Tim and I were discussing his family's background one evening, and it turned out that all was not kosher, so to speak. The conversation went something like this:

"Whereabouts in Natal do you come from, Tim?"

"We farm in Illovo, Southern Natal, and the farm has been in our family for four generations," said he, fairly bursting with pride.

"So, you come from a family dripping in Mercedes, being sugar farmers," I murmured enviously.

"No, no," he replied, "we farm beef and, as meat prices are down, we are struggling a bit at the moment."

There was a long and pregnant silence as I tried to busy myself by adjusting a jib sheet, but eventually I had to ask the obvious question.

"Do you not see any conflict between your vegetarian stance and your profiting from the slaughter of cattle?" asked I, starting to become pro-beef myself.

"Oh, but we don't kill the cattle, we just take them to market," said Tim in a rather smug way that hardened my resolve to make him squirm a little.

"Right, from now on you eat what I eat, or you don't eat at all," I growled in my best Captain Bligh impersonation.

And so it was. We ate normal small-yacht fare, a combination of canned and dried food that would be banned in most European schools today.

***

Sixteen days out of Richards Bay, we were close to the island of Mayotte, a French colonial outpost in the archipelago of the Comores. I decided to put in to the island, try and buy some fresh vegetables, and let us stretch our legs for a few days.

We anchored at Dzaoudzi, and paddled the pram dinghy ashore for what proved to be Tim's first visit to a foreign country, and an incredibly traumatic visit it was.

Firstly, no one spoke English and no amount of gentle admonishment on my part would persuade him that not all French people who spoke no English were retarded at best, seriously imbecilic at worst. I was unlucky enough to witness his treatment of a helpful gendarme whom he had stopped to ask the way.

"Christ! You have got to be kidding! How can you be a cop and not speak English? What is the matter with you people?"

On catching sight of me trying to slip down an alley to hide my embarrassment, he hollered, "Hey John, can you believe that this guy only speaks French?"

No shit, Sherlock.

I had some friends who lived in Mayotte; they were all legionnaires who were stationed with the DLEM, the Détachement de Légion Étrangère de Mayotte, and most of them I knew from previous visits to either Mayotte or Djibouti. They were a hard crowd of fellows; some of them had reached the rank of Adjudant, the highest non-commissioned rank in the French Foreign Legion, and they invited me to a dinner at a venue in the district of Labattoir, a charmingly named area on the isthmus joining the islands of Dzaoudzi and Pamanzi.

The word 'venue' does not really do justice to the patch of mud floor under a tarpaulin where we arrived for the meal. There were six legionnaires including our host, a great bull of a man called Adjudant Philippe, and Tim and me. Philippe's girlfriend, a huge and quivering mountain of Malagasy flesh called Yvette, did not join us for dinner, but kept the food and booze coming at an alarming rate.

This was a proper Legion dinner, so it started with a full bottle of Ricard placed in front of each of us, and a jug of water in the middle of the table. I should add that the 'table' was in fact two doors placed on top of logs of wood, and it was groaning under an assortment of pots on burners, containing such delicacies as curry of fruit bat, chicken kebabs, goat stew, and even some dried lemur meat. Except for the rice and a little sweet potato, there was nothing vegetarian around. Tough luck Tim.

We poured ourselves enormous shots of Ricard, added a little water, lit up rank Gauloise cigarettes, and took it in turns to yell out toasts to each other's countries, to women all over the world, to mercenaries in general, to legionnaires in particular, and to one another. There had been a slight murmur of disapproval when Tim poured only water into his glass, but good manners prevailed for the moment. When the bottles of Ricard had dropped to about a third full, Yvette produced some plates, and the feast was under way, lubricated with large jugs of 'pinard', the rough red wine issued to the Legion.

Philippe realised very quickly that Tim spoke no French, and as none of the legionnaires present spoke English, Philippe made a point of offering Tim every succulent morsel from each pot, and lauded their taste with sign language. The silences grew longer, and the glances at Tim less friendly, until eventually Philippe decided to express what all the guys were thinking.

Yvette poured us each a large tumbler of Madagascar Rum, the sort of drink that should come with a free seeing-eye dog and a white stick and, as usual, Tim refused. Philippe stared at him with a cold and savage look, and attacked. It was my job to translate both sides of the conversation. I felt that something bad was coming.

"Eh bien Tim, tu ne manges pas de viande, tu ne bois pas d'alcool, tu ne fumes pas. Peut-être tu n'aimes pas aussi les femmes?"

I turned to Tim, who had not yet cottoned to the fact that he was in trouble, and translated Philippe's question. Tim flushed, and full of bravado, replied thus.

"Bloody right I like women, I mean I don't smoke and drink because I'm an athlete; I don't eat meat because it's wrong, but I like women alright!"

I explained to Philippe what Tim had said, and a beatific expression spread across his face, he slammed his hand down on the table and bellowed, "Suzanne!"

Yvette's younger sister appeared, about a hundred kilos of simpering sixteen-year-old. She was given swift instructions to take Tim into the sleeping hovel, and not to let him out until she, Suzanne, had screamed for mercy three times.

Tim had watched all this with mounting anxiety and had tried to leave the table, but he was quickly caught and bundled into the room with the giggling Suzanne. He yelled to me piteously, "Please John, tell them that I can't do this, tell them that I'm sick, tell them anything, but get me out!"

I explained that this was not a good time for me to spoil their fun, and I suggested he consider his present situation as part of his education. After some rustling sounds and some high-pitched squeaks from Tim, there was the sound of someone sobbing quietly. Suzanne appeared, teary-eyed, and said she could not understand why the young white boy did not want her.

We sailed from Mayotte the next day, much to Tim's relief and, despite my teasing, he said he would remain vegetarian through all manner of hardship. On arriving in the Seychelles, Tim left the boat, and my non-sailing wife rejoined me for a few weeks, having been promised flat sea and pretty anchorages.

***

I was offered a delivery job in Mahé; the moving of a boat called *Heurtibise* from Mahé to Djibouti, a voyage of about 1700 miles. The boat was a steel ketch of some 40 feet, of a design made famous by Bernard Moitissier, who sailed his *Joshua* around the world non-stop.

I approached young Tim Biggs, who was still in Mahé, and asked if he would like to crew for me again, and he jumped at the idea of a continuing adventure. It was Tim's lucky day: soya mince was cheaper than tinned meat, so a lot of our stores turned out to be vegetarian-friendly. I bought stores for twenty-two days, as I reckoned we would do 100 miles per day, and five days of extra stores was plenty. We sailed north from Mahé at the end of February, not a bad time to leave, as we should be clear of cyclones in the Arabian Sea, and the wind should stay on the starboard beam right up to Cape Guardafui.

I must learn not to take too much notice of those little diagrams in the Pilot volume.

After eighteen days we had not even rounded Cape Guardafui, the Horn of Africa, and we still had another 600 miles to sail. I had started cutting back on food when we were out only ten days, so we were in pretty good shape as far as stores went, and we had plenty of water, having supplemented our tanks with rainwater during the innumerable squalls. Still, we were starting to 'fine down' a bit and, as neither of us carried a lot of fat to begin with, we both looked forward with great interest to the next mealtime. I had motored in the calms as much as I could, but it was prudent to keep some diesel in the tank in case we were becalmed just off Djibouti, so the only motoring that we did during the last 600 miles was while we charged the batteries for about one hour per day.

On entering the Gulf of Aden, the wind all but disappeared and the temperature climbed. We drifted along at ½ knot, or 12 miles per day, the sea like a mirror, and the heat such that we lay under a strip of awning and panted in temperatures of 48-50 degrees Celsius. Sometimes at night there would be a squall or two, and then we would crack on recklessly, often carrying too much sail, but unwilling to slack off for even a single mile.

On the twenty-ninth day at sea, things were becoming quite serious, and although I was not yet looking at Tim as a possible source of nutritious flesh, it did cross my mind that I would never have to worry about him thinking about me that way. I took star sights that evening, and put us just under 100 miles from Djibouti. We were down to two small tins of dehydrated spinach, one of which we had for dinner that night, washed down with a cup of very stale water.

The next morning I was on watch, again ghosting through a flat calm sea, when I saw a flash of gold next to the boat. I watched carefully, and was rewarded with a glimpse of a medium-sized dorado, one of my favourite fish. I ran down below and grabbed the speargun, not bothering to call Tim who was asleep on his bunk. I lay on the side deck, and extended the gun towards the water and, sure enough, the dorado came by again. It was the most terrible shot and I got it through the tail, but the spear held, and I dragged the fish flapping onto the deck, where it went berserk, thumping the deck in its death throes.

Tim appeared in the hatchway, and uttered the most unexpected words, "Oh God John, can we eat it now?" Not bad for a vegetarian.

We did, and I don't think that I have ever enjoyed sushi as much. Tim must have eaten about a kilo of raw fish all on his own, and it was the start of a beautiful relationship between him and seafood.

We found a breeze, and got into Djibouti the next morning, unbelievably fit and healthy, and went our separate ways.

May 1998

Worse Things Happen at Sea

While running a sailing school in Durban on the East coast of South Africa, I had the opportunity to meet some very interesting people and to observe the highest and lowest in some peoples' characters. Mostly, I had a load of fun.

I ran three different courses, and each of them lasted five days. The 'Deckhand' course was designed for the real beginner, and usually started with a short explanation of why a boat floated. The next course was the 'Day Skipper' course, for people who had done the deckhand course, or who had a modicum of experience and wanted to be able to skipper their own little ship. The highest level that anyone could attain at my sailing school then, in 1978, was the 'Coastal Skipper' ticket, which allowed the successful student to sail their boat overnight between ports on the South African coast.

A quick perusal of a chart of the coast will show that there are very few ports, and that they are a good distance apart. This, combined with weather systems that are often terrifying, and a boisterous to sometimes positively evil sea, make the South African coast a very hard training ground for small boat sailors.

Eighty miles to the north of Durban lies the busy commercial port of Richards Bay—not the prettiest harbour, but just inside the port entrance was the Zululand Yacht Club. This was a relaxed and pleasantly sinful little club, where beer flowed at all hours, and husbands and wives seemed to leave their marital vows hanging in the cloakroom. The clubhouse was a two-story affair, with a big veranda around the top floor, and outside ablution blocks next to a small creek.

There was an alarming sign at the creek that read "NO SWIMMING, BEWARE OF SHARKS AND CROCODILES". There was a pleasant green lawn stretching down from the clubhouse to the small dock, and overlooking the small-craft moorings.

I used to start my Coastal Skipper courses with two days of concentrated coastal navigation and tidal work, and then sail up to Richards Bay on the school boat, *Born Free*, for a couple of days, returning to Durban before the weekend. The number of pupils was limited to five, and it was often the first time any of them had spent a night out at sea, so there was usually some excitement and trepidation in the preparations. We would make up a stores list, check the boat over, look at all the emergency equipment, and generally prepare the crew for a much longer voyage than the 80 miles.

The voyage up could take anything from fifteen to thirty hours, depending on the wind direction. We always wished for a southwesterly wind on the way up, and a northeasterly on the way home. Sometimes the wishes came through. The southwesterly wind on the Natal coast normally comes through as a 'buster' and can often blow at 30 to 40 knots for two days, so it makes for lively sailing. The course kept was always close inshore, to avoid the strong southward-flowing Agulhas Current, which sometimes speeds along at 6 knots.

On a particularly memorable trip up to Richards Bay, my motley crew of learners had a pasting on the northbound leg, with heavy rain and a hard beat to windward for the last 20 miles, so we arrived off the Zululand Yacht club very wet and tired. A good feed, a hot shower, and some well-earned beer in the bar soon lightened everyone's spirits, and all enjoyed a calm and restful sleep.

The morning dawned bright and cheerful, and we set to, getting the boat ready for the sail home. The forecast was for moderate northeasterly winds, so we all looked forward to a fast spinnaker run all the way. To this end, I detailed two of the crew to take the medium-weight spinnaker ashore, and to flip it on the grassy lawn before packing it in woollen 'stops' for easy hoisting. By midday we were ready to sail, and motored out into the strengthening wind. I ordered the fellows who had packed the spinnaker to go and prepare it below decks, while the rest led the sheets and guys on deck. We were just about to hoist the sail, when there was an ear-splitting shriek from the fo'c'sle; I rushed below to find one of the crew holding his hand, and going pale enough to pass out, while the other was dancing around like a dervish in his bare feet.

The explanation was bizarre. When they had been flipping the spinnaker on the grass at the yacht club, they must have caught up a scorpion in the sail: a small, black, and very angry scorpion, who obviously disapproved of the gentle art of 'shanghaiing' or being press-ganged into going to sea. The poor fellow who was stung was in a lot of pain, and the other guy had hit his head really hard on the deck head while trying to leap clear of the enraged arachnid.

When all was settled (the scorpion sting with a frozen pack of peas on it), we had the most delightful sail back to Durban, surfing along with a rising moon, and the whole crew agreed: much worse things could happen at sea.

The scorpion? He was allowed to swim ashore.

May 1998

PART FOUR

ENGLISH TALES

A Tale of Gastronomic Horror

The other day I was leaving Lymington by car, heading for Gatwick airport where I would drop off my friend Arne Olsson. Arne had been visiting a shipyard in Lymington, where I was project managing the refit of a unique motor yacht. Arne had looked after the generators on this yacht for the 5 years since launching, and was also a good friend of the owner.

Whenever Arne came to Lymington, we would lunch in one of the excellent pubs in the small town. Arne seems to have low blood sugar, and needs to eat regularly and well.

On this particular Friday, there was a problem with the trains, and it was pouring with rain – what is new about that in England? I decided that we should leave at about 1230, and stop along the way for a decent lunch, we would stop in the New Forest, before we got to the motorway.

I decided on a pub called The Filly, which I had visited with Sune, and where we had enjoyed a great meal. I duly turned into their driveway, to find no lights, no other vehicles, and certainly no warm welcome. Never mind, I thought, there are so many public houses in the area that we were spoiled for choice.

I drove on towards Brockenhurst, happily dreaming of Battered Cod with French fries, (real ones, not the cardboard facsimiles found in cheap eateries), or perhaps an excellent steak and ale pie – real pub fare! In no time at all we arrived at the King and Stirrup, which I had passed many times, and remarked on the large sign outside that said, "GOOD FOOD!" Both Arne and I were salivating at the thought of some good food on our plates, and Arne fairly sprinted through the light rain to the door. Hunger or fear of getting wet?

We entered a cheery bar, a couple of fellows were sitting at the bar and talking to a buxom and cheerful barmaid. I gave her my best smile and asked if we could have a look at the lunch menu. Suddenly she

205

was less cheerful. It seemed that there was a problem in the kitchen, and they were waiting for an engineer.

DISAPPOINTED!!

Arne walked quite slowly to the car, taking no heed of the steady rain. I told him not to worry, we would find something soon, and drove on towards Lyndhurst, the last little town before the motorway.

There we stopped at The Snakecatcher, another hostelry that I had passed and lodged in my memory, determined to visit it sometime. This was quite a busy pub, very low beams, and a delightful atmosphere.

Can you believe it? The cook had called in sick, and no lunch was being served. The visions that I had of Liver and Bacon, possibly a plate of Whitebait, each little fish lightly breaded and flash fried, all disappeared, and again Arne and I splashed through the rain to the car.

Within five miles we were on the motorway, trundling along with the huge trucks, and making the windscreen wipers work at full speed. Arne was very quiet, and I was definitely feeling that there was far too much room between my belt and my stomach. A big blue sign appeared, "ROWAN SERVICES", with various symbols under the lettering, a petrol pump, a bed, and, joy of joys, a crossed knife and fork. Arne gave a low growl, and nodded hopefully, so I took the next off-ramp, and we drove into the forecourt, (oh! The shame of it!), of a McDonalds.

Now, I have never before been inside a McDonalds, and this was going to be a life-changing experience. Arne seemed quite at home in this busy and very plastic environment, he even understood the electronic ordering system, using a large touchscreen, and paying with his credit card. I looked at the crowd of people that were waiting for their meal to be handed to them by one of the legion of kitchen staff, and thought to myself that the food just HAD to be ok, otherwise there would not be a crowd like this here. Right?

Our order arrived quickly, which hinted at the fact that there could not have been a chef in the kitchen, lovingly preparing each meal, but that there was an army of slaves slapping pre-cooked meals into microwave ovens. Our tray arrived with two closed cardboard boxes, two open boxes of quasi-French fries, a little tub of 'sweet curry sauce', and our drinks, a Coke for Arne and hot chocolate for me.

Arne had ordered chicken nuggets, and when he opened the box, there were six articles inside. None of them looked to me as though they bore any relationship whatsoever to something feathery that scratches the ground for a living. He happily dipped ones of these things in the sweet curry sauce and munched away. I cautiously opened my box, and stared in horror at the shiny bun inside. It looked exactly like the fiberglass replica of the meal in the display case in the foyer of the establishment. Under the bun there was a lump of something dark, a piece of processed cheese, a strip of bacon, and a mess of coagulating onions. This was the famous 'BIG MAC'.

I was appalled.

After six or so thousand years of culinary development, the fusing of fascinating cultures from the Far East, Central America, Oceana, and the old world of Europe, is this the result?

I took a small bite of the bun, the bacon, the cheese and the patty (pure beef!). I chewed, and I chewed some more, and eventually I managed to swallow the morsel. Firstly, the patty was certainly not made from any hooved animal that I could recognize, the cheese was indescribable, (possibly one of the slaves in the kitchen had mistaken the wrapper for the cheese), the bacon may have been made from some man-made fiber, and the onions were certainly last years. I swear that if all the lights had gone out, my Big Mac would have glowed in the dark, like some relic from Chernobyl.

I wondered if I was being unfair, so I took another bite and immediately wished that I hadn't. Again, I chewed manfully, until I could swallow the un-nutritious piece of offal. That was it, I was unable to finish my Big Mac. Arne had devoured his radio-active nuggets with gusto, and had finished his fries. I tried a couple of my fries, and yes, they tasted exactly as I imagined the cardboard container would taste. Come to think of it, the container probably had more nutrition in it.

We left McDonalds, and I accelerated away from the portals of the big golden 'M'. I started to feel that I had been poisoned quite soon afterwards, but managed to drop Arne off at Gatwick, drive home to Lymington, and drink two large scotches for medicinal purposes.

I nibbled on a piece of broccoli and had some good Manchego cheese for my dinner, washed down with a glass or two of Cabernet Sauvignon, and headed for bed, worrying about what I had done to my body, and why there were spots swimming before my eyes.

My sleep was racked by terrifying dreams, where little black aliens, dressed as chefs, dragged me screaming towards a huge Golden 'M'.

That is it. Never again, even if close to death by starvation, will I enter one of those hideous houses of malnutrition.

Bon Appetit!

Nativity Play at Primary School

I was once sent a wonderful account of a Nativity Play at a primary school. Unfortunately, I lost it somewhere in cyberspace, I have only vague recollections of the chaos that took place around these beautiful and innocent children. I have tried here to put together the original account, and some of my own ideas of how things could go, when these parasitic little bundles of joy lose the plot and take over the production and performance of something as precious as a Nativity play.

What could be lovelier than a bunch of small children performing a beautiful Christian story, being led into enacting and understanding a wonderful part of religious history?

Nothing.

Unfortunately these things sometimes don't go according to plan, and the blame can seldom be placed at the feet of the benighted primary school teacher, who has given his/her all to produce and manage a small play, normally enacted for the rest of the school and the children's over-appreciative parents.

The Nativity play that I am writing could be played in almost any small, rural or semi-rural area of England. It could, actually, have happened anywhere in the Christian world.

Let us call the producer of the Nativity play Carol. She would be a young woman of around twenty-five years, not with a particularly strong Christian belief, but enough to whole-heartedly take on the task of producing the play. Carol is childless herself, but only because she has not yet found a 'Mr. Right' to father her own offspring. Carol doesn't swear except under the most extreme provocation; she will have a couple of glasses of wine at a festive dinner, but otherwise doesn't drink; she doesn't smoke; and except for the occasional visit from her (usually absent) seaman boyfriend, she is not sexually active.

The raw material that Carol had to work with was not very inspiring. The total number of possible players was fourteen, and of these only twelve were available for the staging of the play (one night only), on the 20th of December. Two members of the small class—twin brothers—had been taken out of school early by their impossible mother for an early skiing holiday. Carol gave a sigh of relief—the brothers were actually young fiends in disguise, and would destroy anything that they could.

The school that Carol teaches at is very progressive, and very politically correct, so there were a couple of children with 'question marks' against their names. The first was little Zvi Zilber, a delightful Jewish child, small for his age and extremely erudite for his six years. The others were a pair of sisters, the children of a Nigerian diplomat. The family was decidedly Muslim, to the point where the little girls came to school each day wearing colourful scarves around their heads.

When Carol received a telephone call from Mr. Zilber, she was surprised that he was insistent that his son had a part, no matter how small, in the play, as he didn't wish that the small Zvi should feel left out. The fact that the play went against Mr. Zilber's religion was insignificant compared to the feeling of exclusion that Zvi had felt when the parts had been assigned.

One small Jewish shepherd, or perhaps a Wise Man?

The Nigerian diplomat phoned Carol, and rumbled the accusation that his daughters were being racially side-lined. Carol, who hated any racial questions, assured the diplomat (an enormous and brooding man with blue-black skin) that the reason his little girls had been left out of the cast was that she, Carol, had worried that it would be taken as a slur against the Muslim faith if the girls were included. The dark and slightly menacing voice on the telephone insisted that his daughters were included, and that they were awarded 'good' parts. Carol stammered an affirmative reply.

Where to put two little girls wearing the hijab?

210

Rehearsal time was at a premium, and there would be opportunities for only two run-throughs and then one dress rehearsal before the great night … well … late afternoon.

The first run-through was fairly disastrous.

The child taking one of the leads, Mary, had taken a violent dislike to the young boy who was the innkeeper. On being told that there was 'no place at the inn', Mary decided to ad-lib, and used language that had certainly not been learned at school. The young innkeeper wilted before this torrent of filthy epithets, and promptly burst into tears.

Carol, when she had regained her breath, tried tactfully to explain that this was not on, and that the script must be adhered to. The beautiful little girl's reply was that her mother had advised her to 'spice it up a bit'. Carol smiled whist silently grinding her teeth and cursing all mothers.

Two of the shepherds had an altercation over their respective positions on the fibreglass and raffia 'hillside', where they were supposed to be watching their 'sheep' (rather obese-looking woolly lambs from a church jumble sale). The problem arose because one of the shepherds, Chris, had two sheep, while the other, Kevin, had only one. The usual battle between capitalism and socialism then erupted, causing the poorer shepherd to whack the richer with his shepherd's crook. Unfortunately, for the sake of realism, and despite Carol's pleas, solid wooden crooks had been used, and the richer shepherd ended up in Matron's care with a bleeding nose and a blackening eye.

There was a wire strung over the stage, on which first the Star of Bethlehem was to be hung, after which the same wire was to be used for the appearance of the Angel Gabriel. All went well, the star didn't fall off the wire and maim a child, and the little boy, Ben, managed his journey through the sky above the stage as the Angel Gabriel (all of eight feet in the air) without screaming in terror.

For the dress rehearsal there was a bit of a hiatus when it was found that little Ben had gone down with chickenpox, so suddenly there was a major part to be filled. The Angel Gabriel was on display for a minimal amount of time and had virtually no dialogue to remember, so Colin, one of the shepherds, was designated for the part. He said very little, and looked a trifle green around the gills when he was fitted with the harness and attached to the wire.

The second run-through was less traumatic.

Mary (played by Colleen) and the innkeeper, Cecil, had made up, but Joseph, played by Brian, had a problem with his bowels, and had to keep running off the stage. This caused great confusion over whose turn it was to speak, and Mary decided to spout Joseph's lines as well as her own.

Carol had a moment of brilliance, and cast young Zvi as Balthazar, and the two Nigerian sisters, Tyra and Courtney, as Melchior and Gaspar – a blow struck for feminism! The three 'Kings' were to be dressed very richly, and all three wore coloured cloaks with hoods, so the wearing of the hijabs wasn't a problem. All the shepherds had the same grey coloured cloaks, which covered whatever the children were wearing. Gabriel wore a long white sort of nightgown, with rather unlikely wings sewn onto the back. Colin was instructed to wear clean white underpants which wouldn't show through the material.

Carol had decided to go a little avant-garde with her choice of soundtracks, and there was a compilation of traditional Christmas carols, mixed in with some more modern stuff. It was noticed that each time the Bony M rendition of 'Mary's Boy Child' was played, Melchior and Gaspar were inclined to go back to their roots and 'bop', with much roiling of hips and other motions not required in a Nativity play.

Carol made sure that they understood that this must stop.

The big day arrived, and the school hall was packed with parents, older children and most of the village, including the vicar, a couple of councillors, and the local police sergeant. Carol was in the wings, making sure that her charges were all prepped and comfortable with their lines. There was great excitement, and it was with relief that the time arrived when there was nothing more to do.

A lovely little girl called Jessica marched to the centre of the stage, and started to lisp the prologue of the story, only breaking concentration once, when she spied her proud parents in the audience, waved, and with a beautiful smile, yelled "Hallo Mummy and Daddy!"

Carol closed her eyes, and prayed very hard.

Jessica moved over to the left side of the stage and started to read the story as the various players appeared. All was going swimmingly until Joseph (Brian), had a complete memory loss, and in the deafening silence he did what he always did in moments of stress. He picked his nose. Carol watched in horror as the little boy's entire forefinger disappeared into his nostril, while Mary (Colleen), happily took centre stage and recited his lines for him. This in turn confused the innkeeper, who was not up to the task of sorting out who was supposed to say what, so he marched off the stage.

Carol was beside herself, and then things got worse. There was a shout from the audience, as a parent told his offspring to "behave yourself". Carol directed her vision towards something unpleasant on the 'hillside', where one of the shepherds had divested himself of his cloak, and, resplendent in a Spiderman costume, seemed to be doing something rather unhealthy to his woolly lamb.

"Oh fuck!" Breathed Carol. Everything was going wrong. Perhaps the show would be saved by the dramatic appearance of Gabriel.

The Star had done it's crossing of the stage to oohs and aahs from the audience, the three Kings had appeared on cue, with Zvi leading the presentation of the gifts of gold, frankincense and myrrh, and things seemed to be running ok. The soundtrack came to the Bony M number, and sure enough, Melchior and Gaspar started to bop, only stopping when Carol hit the fast forward on the sound machine.

The big moment arrived and Jessica said the magic words, "And the Angel Gabriel appeared," in her sweet lisping voice. There was a strangled sound from young Colin, who had been hitched to the overhead wire with his harness back-to-front, so as he swooped above the stage, he was vainly trying to turn around to face the spellbound audience. The more he tried to turn, the harder it became for the sports master in the wings to pull him along the wire. He eventually stopped, jammed solid, above the now complete crowd surrounding the crib. With a monumental effort, Colin swung half round, but the movement had unforeseen and unfortunate results.

To Carol's horror, Colin first farted extremely loudly, and in his terror and embarrassment, he lost control of his bladder. The gentle rain that fell onto the party around the crib was at first not recognized for what it was. But when it was, there were cries of consternation. Colin just hung there in his harness, and the sports master was able to slide him out of sight into the wings.

Mary, Joseph, the three Kings and one unlucky shepherd all ran off the stage shrieking with disgust. The rest of the shepherds followed in great confusion, dragging their woolly lambs. Little Jessica, with great presence of mind, lisped "The End!" and beamed at the audience. Applause slowly started, and then increased in tempo, while the vicar was seen to brush tears from his eyes.

Carol later sat down with a bottle of wine, and told her fellow teachers that never, ever again would she agree to run the Nativity play.

But then she said that every year.

Merry Christmas!!

December 2015

Printed in Poland
by Amazon Fulfillment
Poland Sp. z o.o., Wrocław